D1509077

ADDITIONAL PRAISE FOR
PROCUREMENT 20/20

"Shaping new products through early involvement, bringing outside perspectives to better design a company's value chain, or fully managing a company's outsourcing network—the expectations for CPOs are rising constantly. *Procurement 20/20* compellingly explains what CPOs should expect, and how they can shape the future."

—Fredrick Spalcke, EVP Procurement, Philips

"*Procurement 20/20* provides valuable insights into the impact globalization and volatility will have throughout the value chain. Leaders will benefit in understanding how these factors and others will shape their sourcing strategies today and into the future."

—Michael Radojevic, Managing Director of Technology and Corporate Services Procurement, United Airlines

"In today's fast changing world, managing to a benchmark is important but simply not enough. Future development and trends have to be anticipated and management adjusted accordingly. In this spirit *Procurement 20/20* is an excellent resource for any CPO. It provides compelling visions for the future of the function and hands-on solutions for a challenging business environment. A must read!"

—Rüdiger Eberhard, CPO, Evonik

"*Procurement 20/20* looks beyond the classical sourcing tasks and explores how to establish strategic business models with the supply base, reduce risks, and drive growth to create more value along a company's full value chain. An inspiring thought-piece for any procurement professional."

—Albie van Buel, CPO, Vestas Wind

"We aspire to mastering all opportunities offered by the rapidly changing marketplace, and this book provides an excellent road map for the journey that lies ahead of us."

—Hans Melotte, Vice President and Chief Procurement Officer, Johnson & Johnson

"*Procurement 20/20* takes a bold look into the future and explores the changes that the procurement function needs to make. It is a must read for the ambitious CPO."

—Babara Kux, Member of the Managing Board, Siemens AG

"The next decade will require the procurement function to better understand the dynamic and volatile world, particularly where sourcing strategies must be flexible and creative to operate in a global footprint. This book provides the CPO and the procurement team with several provocative trends that will shape the coming years, and a structured road map to address the opportunities."

—*Luiz Lissoni, Vice President
of Supply Chain, Brasil Foods*

"*Procurement 20/20* is an inspiring invitation to stop and reflect on the 'new normal' for procurement. And it sends a clear message to CPOs: It's time to get ready for the next decade!"

—*Bertrand Conqueret, CPO, Henkel*

"This book explores very convincingly how CPOs and their organizations need to adapt to deal with the challenges of the future."

—*Vicente San Miguel, Chief Procurement Officer, Telefónica*

"A highly inspiring book: The strategic insights draw the necessary change agenda for all CPOs. It is written in a most engaging style, provides numerous examples relevant to today's world, establishes the burning platform, and outlines the key elements that the new procurement agenda must address. If there ever was a book to motivate the CPO to action, this is it!"

—*Alan Hustwick, CPO, Pacific Aluminium*

"Today's global megatrends make the strategic side of procurement increasingly vital for the success of any business, from strategic supply management to sourcing innovation. A revealing book on supply entrepreneurship."

—*Paul van Attekum, EVP Supply
Management, ASML*

"A must-read for practitioners and academics alike."

—*Christian Terwiesch, Andrew M. Heller Professor
at the Wharton School of the University of Pennsylvania*

Procurement 20/20

Procurement 20/20

Supply Entrepreneurship in a Changing World

PETER SPILLER
NICOLAS REINECKE
DREW UNGERMAN
HENRIQUE TEIXEIRA

WILEY

Cover Design: Wiley
Cover Image, top: © iStockphoto/traffic_analyzer
Cover Image, bottom: © iStockphoto/krystiannawrocki

Published by John Wiley & Sons, Inc., Hoboken, New Jersey.
Published simultaneously in Canada.

For general information on our other products and services or for technical support, please contact our Customer Care Department within the United States at (800) 762-2974, outside the United States at (317) 572-3993 or fax (317) 572-4002.

Wiley publishes in a variety of print and electronic formats and by print-on-demand. Some material included with standard print versions of this book may not be included in e-books or in print-on-demand. If this book refers to media such as a CD or DVD that is not included in the version you purchased, you may download this material at http://booksupport.wiley.com. For more information about Wiley products, visit www.wiley.com.

Library of Congress Cataloging-in-Publication Data:

Spiller, Peter, 1972–
    Procurement 20/20 : supply entrepreneurship in a changing world / Peter Spiller, Nicolas Reinecke, Drew Ungerman, Henrique Teixeira.
      pages cm
    Includes index.
    ISBN 978-1-118-80008-9 (cloth); ISBN 978-1-118-80047-8 (ebk);
    ISBN 978-1-118-80070-6 (ebk)
      1. Industrial procurement.   I. Title.
  HD39.5.S6866   2014
  658.7'2—dc23

          2013038860

Printed in the United States of America
10 9 8 7 6 5 4 3 2

Contents

Preface   *ix*

Introduction: The Procurement Advantage   *xiii*

PART 1   **FROM GOOD TO GREAT PROCUREMENT**   **1**

CHAPTER 1   The Drivers of Sustainable Procurement Performance   3

Procurement pays. Yet there is no free lunch in obtaining procurement excellence. The best companies pay for talent, and advanced procurement tools and strategies become essential to achieve cost savings. Long-term success can lead to a strategic role for procurement teams and a seat on the board for CPOs.

CHAPTER 2   The Megatrends That Impact Competitive Advantage   15

Five megatrends are impacting virtually every company doing business in the global economy—in particular, the procurement strategies of those companies. Do you know what those megatrends are and how they will touch you? If not, read on. Reacting and adapting to these megatrends will be essential to procurement flexibility and competitive advantage by the end of this decade.

PART 2   **RESPONDING TO THE MEGATRENDS OF THE NEXT DECADE**   **29**

CHAPTER 3   The Great Global Rebalancing: Building a Dynamic Sourcing Footprint   31

Sourcing-footprint decisions have a short half-life. They have to accommodate everything from best-cost suppliers to regulatory challenges and unprecedented risks. Trickier still is that the relative influence of these factors changes constantly. Are you ready to respond dynamically? And in doing so, can you help other functions advance their own global footprints?

CHAPTER 4   The Productivity Imperative: Orchestrating the
                  End-to-End Value Chain   49

Successful companies seamlessly manage their end-to-end value
chain and tightly orchestrate a network of internal functions and
external providers to best serve their customers. What role is procurement playing in this game? How can you take the pivotal
orchestrator role?

CHAPTER 5   Big Data and the Global Grid: Procurement's
                  New Role in Data-Driven Decision Making   73

Two related developments—big data and the global grid—are
combining to dramatically alter procurement's possibilities. Sitting
right on top of the various data streams between the company
and its external vendors and partners, procurement must find
ways to analyze, structure, interpret, and apply the abundance of
data on markets and suppliers to decision-making problems. How
are you preparing to seize the resulting opportunities?

CHAPTER 6   Volatility as the New Normal: Translating Sourcing
                  Risk into Competitive Advantage   91

Procurement operates amid growing volatility and persistent
uncertainty. To protect against—or even benefit from—this challenging context, leading organizations are becoming agile. What
does this mean in practice? And how can procurement use agility
to create a competitive advantage?

CHAPTER 7   The New Economic Drivers: Capturing the
                  Total Impact of Environmental, Social,
                  and Regulatory Factors   117

Environmental, social, and regulatory considerations are poised
to become key decision-making variables for CPOs as they select
suppliers of goods and services. What are some of the innovative
solutions that leading procurement organizations are experiment-
ing with in order to cope?

PART 3   **THE ROAD MAP TO
                  PROCUREMENT 20/20**   **137**

CHAPTER 8   Getting Ready for Real Change: Steps for Starting the
                  Journey toward Procurement 20/20   139

Going for Procurement 20/20 is a stretch aspiration. If you are up
for it, your successful transformation should place equal emphasis

on two elements: your company's business performance and its organizational health. It's a tricky balance to strike. Discover how to do it.

CHAPTER 9   Your Agenda Now   157

Seizing the opportunities we've discussed means moving from supply management to supply entrepreneurship. The time for visible and tangible action has arrived. What's your plan of action?

About the Authors   *159*

Acknowledgments   *161*

Index   *163*

Preface

For decades, McKinsey & Company has worked with clients to improve their procurement practices and achieve distinctive and sustainable impact. We have averaged more than 250 engagements per year and served chief procurement officers (CPOs) from Fortune 100 companies and start-ups alike. Those companies have come from industries ranging from automotive and assembly, chemicals and basic materials, electronics and high tech to energy, banking, and other services. Many of them have been long-standing clients, served on a broad range of strategic and operational topics, and a large share we have been advising at different procurement inflection points over time: when a new CPO came on board, a merger required significant synergy contributions from procurement, a general reorganization offered the opportunity to strengthen the central procurement governance, or when new sourcing markets had to be explored.

In working with our clients on these engagements, we have been exposed to the most important questions faced by CEOs and CPOs around the world—such as how do we develop cutting-edge sourcing strategies, exploit favorable market conditions, and optimize supply chains to reduce cost across the value chain? How do we build a base of external suppliers that give us the first access to their proprietary innovations so that we can jointly develop the products consumers want, more profitably and more quickly? How do we manage a vast and complex network of suppliers and contract manufacturers to ensure constant supply in a world where supply chains are globalizing, lengthening, and susceptible to more volatility? And how do we make our procurement practices robust enough to avoid the increasing scrutiny of environmental, safety, and regulatory demands, magnified by vastly different expectations from a diverse set of consumers and governments?

This book shares the hard-earned insights from more than 10 years of dedicated procurement research conducted with leading academic institutions and practical experience with marquee clients in the field of procurement and is the natural successor to the many articles we have published on the topic. As such, we've attempted two things with this book: to explain and codify the best practices that leading companies have pioneered in procurement and to frame how procurement must evolve to grapple with new global, social, and economic issues affecting business over the next decade. We wanted it to be as forward thinking and strategic as you've learned to expect from our publications, yet practical enough to spark a conversation between a CEO and CPO about the near-term actions their procurement organizations must take to stay ahead in the new world. And while this book is focused on procurement, any company executive—from CEO to COO to CPO—will find relevance in our discussion of the five major megatrends that will impact every function across the business.

Why are we devoting an entire book to procurement excellence today and how it must evolve to be ready for tomorrow? We look at procurement's past evolution for an answer. In his 1983 article "Purchasing Must Become Supply Management," our former colleague Peter Kraljic noted, "A decade ago, any chief executive who was losing sleep over his company's procurement function might be thought to have had his priorities wrong. Today, the likelihood is that he is simply more alert than his competitors to the new and potentially dangerous strategic dimension that materials sourcing has taken on." As a result, Kraljic argued, procurement must transition from a tactical, operational mind-set to one that is strategic and fully integrated with other key functions in the business.[1] Even back then, Kraljic argued that procurement could deliver significant impact by responding to the increasing risks of resource depletion and raw-material scarcity, intensified competition, political turbulence and government intervention in supply markets, and accelerating technological change. In fact, the past 10 years have provided a natural conclusion to what Kraljic predicted: The digitalization of information spread the news of the 2008 Lehman Brothers bankruptcy in seconds, causing world stock exchanges to plunge simultaneously and putting companies out of business; the 2011 Japanese earthquake and tsunami sent reverberations across global supply chains; and the 2010–2011 Arab Spring resulted in instability and speculation across the most oil-rich region in the world. The decade ahead will be no less tumultuous, and procurement's role will be more important than ever before in maintaining constant supply, best cost, reduced volatility, faster and improved innovation, and positive corporate-brand image. Our purpose is to take Kraljic's view deep into the twenty-first century by describing the next step in the evolution, the step in which *supply management must become supply entrepreneurship*.

Toward that goal, we have brought to bear our insights, which have, time and again, proven their entrepreneurial and strategic effectiveness as

---

[1]Peter Kraljic, "Purchasing Must Become Supply Management," *Harvard Business Review*, September/October 1983.

our external partners compete in the global economy. We have drawn on more than 1,500 global procurement studies from the past five years that optimized in excess of U.S. $200 billion of spend, examinations of more than 700 procurement organizations, and 2,000 hours of interviews with CPOs and their staffs across every industry to determine the key dimensions of procurement excellence and its link to corporate performance. The research presented in this book is unique because of the challenges inherent in measuring the success of a single company function. Enlisting top academic institutions, we have developed a framework to isolate the performance and impact of a single business function and to evaluate its impact with a very high confidence level using partial least squares (PLS) statistical methods and multiple-level blind interviews. This framework is, in our view, unrivaled in its detail and provides essential insights for other organizations seeking to remain competitive into the future. The McKinsey Global Institute, our business and economic research arm, has partnered with our strategy practice to identify the five fundamental megatrends that will shape the next decade and beyond. On the basis of the implications of these megatrends, we have tapped into our global network of C-suite officers across leading companies to help define how procurement must evolve. And finally, we've drawn on our organization practice to provide practical advice on how to accomplish transformational change—from defining the aspirations to executing them so that they become part of your function's DNA.

Numerous executives and companies were involved in the development of this book. In particular, we would like to thank the more than 700 clients who took part in our Global Purchasing Excellence survey and served as the inspiration behind the disguised case examples that bring to life the concepts in this book. We would also like to thank the many CPOs who have shared their insights on the book's content during roundtables and conferences and on a one-on-one basis, ensuring it is simultaneously inspirational, relevant, and actionable.

Hindsight is 20/20, and in 10 years, we'll have the benefit of knowing much more than we do today. And at that point, our hope is that you might be browsing your library or your tablet and thinking, "I'm glad I read this."

Let the journey to Procurement 20/20 begin.

PETER SPILLER
NICOLAS REINECKE
DREW UNGERMAN
HENRIQUE TEIXEIRA

McKinsey & Company
Purchasing and Supply Management Practice

Introduction: The
Procurement Advantage

It is becoming more and more important for every senior executive to know how to manage the external parts of the company's value chain.

The evidence is all around us. Look at the news headlines and the experiences you or others in your organization have faced in recent years. Natural disasters and scarcities of raw materials have exacerbated volatility in supply chains, disrupted operations, and caused significant swings in input pricing. As one example, Honda had to weather a tripling of its raw material index between 2009 and 2012; was hit hard by the tsunami in Japan and floods in Thailand, causing a 59 percent profit drop; and has to deal with business-endangering materials scarcity, for example in some specific rare earths like lanthanum. External functional specialists—contract manufacturers and third-party logistics providers, to name just two categories—have proliferated, in both the developed and the emerging worlds, and they regularly deliver new levels of innovation and efficiency up and down the value chain. And yet increasingly stringent ethical, social, and governmental requirements mean that if those specialists have a slipup, it can spoil the brand image of the company whose procurement organization is sourcing from them.

The data further prove the point. Across all the companies listed in Standard & Poor's 500 stock index, external spend as a fraction of total cost has increased by an average of 40 percent since 1970. Specifically, it has grown from roughly 60 percent of a company's total expenditure in 1970 to an average of 85 percent in 2010. This is true across sectors as disparate as health care, industrials, banks, and energy. Looking at external spend as a fraction of total revenues reveals the same trend: an increase of more than 30 percent over the past 40 years.

In parallel with this increase of external spend, the employees of those companies have been expected to deliver more. In 1970, companies on the S&P 500 were realizing $40,000 in revenues per employee (RPE). That value has risen almost 22-fold, to roughly $900,000 per employee. Seems like a radical shift? Absolutely. And yet this radical shift is not a one-off occurrence—it is seen across both successful and trailing industries, and industry leaders and laggards alike. Take information technology (IT) industry giant Apple, which brought in roughly $1,700,000 in revenues per employee in 2011, despite hiring an astounding 30 percent more employees in just the previous year. While seemingly much higher than fellow player Hewlett-Packard (HP), at $360,000 RPE, HP's RPE has increased a whopping 17-fold since 1970, showing the same focus on greater employee efficiencies. Dow Chemical Company, FMC Corporation, and DuPont, all diversified chemicals players, saw increases in RPE of from 16-fold to 29-fold. Even struggling industries, like automotive, saw companies like Ford bring in over $800,000 per employee, for a 24-fold increase.

The implication is clear: The ways in which the procurement function manages its external spending can confer enormous competitive advantage.

In fact, our research demonstrates that best-practice procurement consistently lowers costs, freeing funds for growth initiatives. Our seven-year Global Purchasing Excellence (GPE) survey of more than 700 companies, across every sector, found that, in total, the participating companies generate U.S. $84 billion in annual cost savings every year. GPE participants were divided into three groups—leaders, average performers, and followers—on the basis of their average overall performance across the criteria in the survey. The leaders not only generated higher cost savings from procurement—30 percent more than average performers—but they also performed better against a broader set of indicators, reducing their cost of goods sold four times faster and achieving higher overall returns from operations. The procurement followers have the highest potential for improvement: Catching up with the leaders would more than double their annual cost savings. The research also shows that opportunities for leveraging procurement exist in all industries—in fact, performance differences among companies in the same industry were much wider than differences among whole industries. Even in industries known for their weak procurement practices, such as financial institutions and utilities, we have found strong procurement leaders that stack up to the best automotive leaders.

The call to action is all too clear. CEOs must hold their chief procurement officers (CPOs) accountable on two levels. CEOs have to demand programs that, in short order, bring procurement practices much closer to those of today's top performers, focusing on traditional levers to achieve significant cost savings and performance improvement. And they must look to their CPOs to successfully exploit the value offered by a growing external supply base, in the context of the opportunities and risks of the decade to come. The issue in both cases is timing—any transformation, and in particular a cross-functional transformation, takes time to achieve because each one requires a mind-set change by a broad set of employees.

And actions must be taken soon. For many companies, the world is changing uncomfortably fast. A few snapshots: Google—not long ago just a convenient web search-engine company—has taken technology to the next level by pioneering the driverless car, which has the potential to revolutionize the auto industry and transportation infrastructure. In 2011, Latin American and Eastern European companies opened more outsourcing facilities than were opened in India, capitalizing on the time zone and multilingual opportunities to service North American and European customers, respectively. The U.S. government debt has surpassed $16 trillion as public policy expands to provide wider social safety nets and universal health care. And the Libyan revolution sparked a mad dash for power over oil reserves, even though that nation accounts for only 2 percent of the world's oil supplies.

As disparate as these occurrences might seem, they all have significant implications for how the field of procurement must evolve to lead—in an entrepreneurial spirit—in this new world. Are CEOs and CPOs discussing these implications? More important, are they ready for them?

This book is designed to help inform and enrich those conversations—and in some cases to initiate them. Here is a quick overview of each chapter and its purpose:

> Chapter 1, "The Drivers of Sustainable Procurement Performance," dives into the four key dimensions of procurement excellence we uncovered through our GPE survey. This is essential reading for CPOs who want to understand how their organizations stack up against these foundational elements and who welcome practical advice for how to close the gap with the best practices described.
>
> Chapter 2, "The Megatrends That Impact Competitive Advantage," showcases the five megatrends that will change the way business is done in the next decade. It draws heavily on research from the McKinsey Global Institute and our Strategy practice. This chapter should have a profound impact on how every senior executive thinks—not only about the company's procurement function but also about its entire operations, sales and marketing, IT, and external-relations activities.
>
> Chapters 3 through 7 form the heart of the book and constitute its second major part, "Responding to the Megatrends of the Next Decade." Each provides a detailed exploration of the profound impact of one of the megatrends that will have a major impact on companies as a whole and on procurement in particular. Throughout, we provide strategies that business leaders can adopt in the face of these trends, together with practical advice about next steps and case examples for inspiration. Chapter 3,

"The Great Global Rebalancing," explores the implications of the rise of developing economies and especially how Western companies need to adapt by building a dynamic sourcing footprint. Chapter 4, "The Productivity Imperative," illustrates how companies can create productivity gains by designing and orchestrating their business as an end-to-end value chain, consisting of internal and external parties. Chapter 5, "Big Data and the Global Grid," highlights the opportunities presented by superior, data-driven decision making at the interface to a company's supply base. Chapter 6, "Volatility as the New Normal," explains how companies can translate sourcing risk into competitive advantage. And finally, Chapter 7, "The New Economic Drivers," explores how sourcing decision-making processes will have to increasingly reflect environmental, social, and regulatory factors.

Our final part, "The Road Map to Procurement 20/20," is designed to prepare your procurement organization for the changes that the preceding chapters have indicated are necessary. These chapters, "Getting Ready for Real Change" and "Your Agenda Now," provide the framework and give practical advice for redefining your vision for procurement and implementing the required changes.

We cannot predict which chapters will resonate most with your executive team and your procurement organization; everyone's situation is, of course, unique. But we do believe that the chapters' collective contents add up to a message you cannot afford to ignore.

Procurement 20/20

PART 1

From Good to Great Procurement

The Drivers of Sustainable Procurement Performance

D oes my procurement organization already employ best-in-class practices, sophisticated tools with the right talent, and the necessary formal and informal cross-functional linkages?

Some 50 to 90 percent of the companies that answer this question will respond "no." On the one hand, this realization is a good indication of readiness for change and the acceptance that development is needed. On the other hand, though, these organizations should realize not only that they are missing an opportunity today but also that they will not have the basic building blocks in place to be ready for the challenges that the next decade will bring.

How do we know that the gap is so large? Over the past five years, McKinsey & Company has conducted more than 1,500 global procurement studies. And we have also examined more than 700 procurement organizations in detail and spent more than 2,000 hours interviewing chief procurement officers (CPOs) and their staff members. The result of this Global Purchasing Excellence (GPE) research is an in-depth examination of the links between procurement health and corporate performance.

The findings confirm that procurement pays: Companies with high-performing procurement functions consistently outperform their rivals on a range of financial indicators, and the best companies are building advanced talent-management strategies into the very heart of their procurement organizations.

So why is not everyone capturing the value at hand? Often, the reasons are quite trivial: lack of talent, overhead cost pressures, unclear governance, and insufficient systems and data. The research we conducted clearly shows that not paying attention to procurement is a significant lapse of judgment. While many reasons are indeed significant management challenges, the impact achieved with good procurement far outweighs the efforts needed to overcome them.

In this chapter, we discuss how procurement pays across all industries, and we detail the key drivers for procurement success.

Procurement Pays

High-performing procurement functions deliver huge value to their companies. This is the case regardless of industry. In addition to the U.S. $84 billion (cumulative) in yearly cost savings cited earlier, procurement leaders deliver superior returns from their operations, as well as lower cost of goods sold.

Our research confirms that every industry has its high performers in procurement. But we also find significant variations in performance among companies within an industry—much wider, in fact, than the performance differences between industries.

Of those companies surveyed in the energy and utilities industry, for example, only 11 percent were considered to be procurement leaders, delivering a GPE score greater than 3 (1 = low, 5 = high), while a whopping 40 percent were rated as procurement followers—that is, those whose performance was below the average for the total sample (see Exhibit 1.1). Even in the automotive and assembly industry, long considered a model of advanced procurement performance, only 51 percent were ranked as procurement leaders. It's clear that there is plenty of room for improvement across all industries.

Our data on the spread of procurement performance across industries provide compelling evidence that an effective corporate procurement function generates significant and sustainable value. As one CEO we interviewed put it, echoing the views of many others, "The profit lies in purchasing now—and even more so in the future."

The same GPE research points to four key dimensions that enable best-practice procurement organizations to stand apart:

1. **Capabilities and culture**—defined as the way that procurement professionals think, plan, conduct themselves in the workplace, and communicate, individually and collectively.
2. **Category management and execution**—that is, the procurement strategies and processes that the company follows in order to create value.
3. **Structures and systems**—meaning how the organization manages the procurement function's resources through formal and informal structures and how the function interacts with other company functions.

Spread of procurement performance, by industry

Average score of industry group

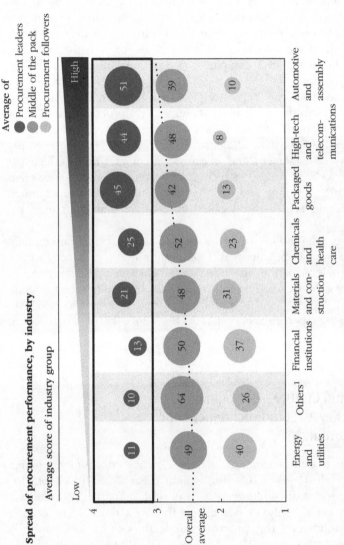

Average of
- ● Procurement leaders
- ● Middle of the pack
- ● Procurement followers

Average procurement practice score (scale 1 = low, 5 = high)
Size of each bubble represents share within its group (%).

EXHIBIT 1.1 There Are Procurement Leaders in Every Industry

[1] Including retail, travel and logistics, services, entertainment, and public sector.

Source: McKinsey Global Purchasing Excellence.

5

4. **Integration and alignment**—defined as procurement's alignment with and support of the overall business strategy.

The best procurement organizations excel along each of these four core dimensions. But it is essential to point out that one dimension in particular—capabilities and culture—is the key to driving procurement health and the strength of the bottom line. It correlates 1.5 to 2.2 times more strongly with the health of a company's procurement function than does any other dimension.

At the same time, capabilities and culture have an important, two-way relationship with the other three dimensions: a procurement function needs the right talent to achieve its key objectives, but it also adopts an approach to each of the core dimensions that optimizes the use of that talent. Category management and execution are much more effective if executed by excellent people. Structure and systems cater to excellent people by creating leverage and exposure. And integration and alignment are much easier to achieve with outstanding talent than with mediocre personnel.

In one case, the CPO of a global logistics and transportation company set out to improve his procurement organization's performance, focusing exclusively on talent for the first three years. He spent his time "recruiting the right people, developing the right skills, and building an appetite for real impact," he recalled. "Everything else came a distant second." The result? Double-digit percentage cost reductions in each of the following three years!

Capabilities and Culture—Recognizing Talent as the Key Asset in Procurement and Investing Accordingly

The most effective procurement practices make enormous demands on the people whose job it is to implement them. Of all those on procurement leaders' staff, 40 percent are educated to the postgraduate level, compared with only 14 percent of those on the staff of companies rated as followers. But procurement leaders don't look only for high educational attainment. They also look for attitude and ability, recognizing how much harder it is to change an employee's hardwired attitudes than it is to develop function-specific capabilities. The best organizations select "supply entrepreneurs"—high-performing individuals who are ready and willing to take full ownership for their categories and to push boundaries as if they were spending their own money.

These profiles are business-oriented and aligned with the requirements that were articulated by other business functions, such as sales and marketing and business development, several decades ago. The CPO of a global conglomerate summarized it this way: "I hire for attitude and train for skill."

The training programs used by procurement leaders are both broader and deeper than those of the others. While nearly all companies in our research train their people in core procurement skills such as negotiation, the procurement leaders also offer training in more advanced skills such as sourcing-strategy development, advanced analytics, and the structured identification of category-specific improvement levers. Furthermore, they build more general business, leadership, and intercultural skills among their strategic procurement personnel.

That is just the start. Procurement leaders build on these training programs by building experience: They deliberately rotate staff both within procurement and across functions. For example, 70 percent of the procurement leaders run internal job-rotation programs (with the majority of program participants moving into higher-level positions), whereas only 29 percent of the average performers do so. In many cases, these rotation programs keep category managers in their positions for only three years and have them rotate to other functions after five or six years.

During their job-rotation programs, the leaders work hard to balance the outflow and inflow of talent by earmarking capable individuals to return to the purchasing functions. In this way, they avoid excessive brain drain. All in all, their efforts make procurement an important career stepping-stone.

Talented people are also rewarded for outstanding performance. The bonuses offered by procurement leaders are both higher and harder to get than those offered by followers. For example, high-level strategic procurement staff at leading procurement organizations have a maximum potential bonus of approximately 45 percent of their base salary, while at procurement's average performers, the comparable figure is only 30 percent.

Category Management and Execution—Improving Effectiveness through Advanced Procurement Tools and Approaches

Category management is the fundamental driver of procurement value, and the best organizations ensure that their category management machinery is both powerful and effective. Power comes from high-caliber staff: Procurement leaders invest 29 strategic full-time equivalent (FTE) employees per U.S. \$1 billion in spending, compared with just 17 FTEs at purchasing followers. The return on these investments is typically between 15 and 25 times the cost. (That is, they earn their salary by mid-January or, in dollar equivalents, there is a \$20 million to \$30 million impact created by 12 additional FTEs.) Purchasing leaders also extend the influence of the procurement function to ensure that more of the company's overall spend is controlled by procurement. At procurement leaders, the average figure is 82 percent compared with 65 percent for procurement followers. The leaders are heavily involved in procurement of nontraditional categories such as marketing and capital expenditure.

Effectiveness is ensured through excellence in execution. Strong procurement organizations share an unflinching focus on process standardization, but they are careful not to let a dogmatic adherence to standards detract from performance. They develop standards for building a procurement function in which everyone works as one team, speaks the same business language, rotates freely among roles and categories, and measures success in common terms. But at the same time, staff members in these organizations have the freedom to adapt to the specific needs of particular categories, markets, and projects, tweaking or creating new standards to ensure that the most effective approaches are absorbed into the fabric of the organization.

Great tools matter, too. Procurement leaders exploit the explosion in data digitalization and improved analytics to make extensive use of selected e-procurement tools such as electronic purchasing catalogs and spend analysis software. However, contrary to common belief, they tend to do this for efficiency and not for effectiveness—another indication of the value and scarcity of talent.

At the same time, information technology (IT) is important in high-performing organizations, and it will become even more important. Among procurement leaders, almost three-quarters scored "very good" or better in e-literacy. They consistently use their IT solutions to speed and simplify transactional and administrative work, freeing up their staff to add more value.

The leading companies participating in our GPE research also encourage their staff to pursue value beyond basic commercial levers, through demand and specification management. Hence, procurement leaders make widespread use of the total-cost-of-ownership methodology, best-cost country sourcing, and design-to-value management. It was, for example, the new CPO, not the head of engineering, at one of our globally leading high-tech clients who launched a comprehensive design-to-cost-and-value program addressing all global businesses and product lines over a two-year period. Financial impact from redesigning products and supply chains, defeaturing, and managing sourcing demand down reached 20 percent in the majority of the businesses touched—a very significant value creation attributed to the procurement leadership. Approaches like this help buoy the entrepreneurial attitude that procurement leaders have consciously cultivated among their staff members, creating much more impact across the organization.

Structure and Systems—Organizing for Economies of Skill

The significance of a center-led procurement function is clear from the research data. Of the procurement leaders, 95 percent have a fully centrally coordinated procurement organization or a hybrid model that combines a center-led structure with some decentralized elements. Contrast this with procurement followers: 25 percent have no centrally coordinated procurement function. This seems surprising to most observers, given that the economies of scale are often small and balanced with the proximity to the internal customer. However, economies of scale are less relevant because only 25 percent of the impact is commercial, while specification and demand management drive 75 percent of impact. For specification and demand management, economies of skill—not economies of scale—are relevant, another indication of the value of talent.

In fact, the top-performing companies participating in the research most often choose organizational structures that build on economies of skill. They centralize strategically important tasks and delegate many of their tactical procurement activities. Their best staff members are given the most important work—tasks such as defining the overall sourcing strategy and negotiating framework agreements.

Leading companies also excel at internal collaboration—with procurement at the center of the action. Their procurement organizations regularly extend their efforts beyond cost reduction and supply chain performance, measuring a combination of price, quality, and supply chain performance and striving for other strategic goals—for example, access to intellectual property. None of this happens without a cross-functional, collaborative approach. Almost all procurement leaders report extensive collaborative activities with internal customers, whereas less than one-third of followers say that is the case. The collaboration can be as simple as closely and early on aligning on the specific internal customer sourcing needs that procurement has to act upon or as complex as jointly developing extensive category strategies that may explore make-or-buy and outsourcing matters or new supplier development opportunities. In any case, there is a clear link between cross-functional collaboration and procurement excellence, as most procurement levers explicitly require the engagement of functions outside procurement.

Another way to maximize economies of skill is to ensure that best practices, once established, are shared widely across the organization. Our research revealed that procurement leaders have effective knowledge-management processes in place to capture, codify, and communicate the best practices. Siemens, for example, centrally collects and maintains clearly defined procurement practices, processes, and methods and facilitates extensive sharing and application in all global businesses. This starts with a uniform definition of spend baselines, targets, and savings types across businesses as diverse as power plants and hearing aids, and extends to the joint pursuit of supplier development or efficiency initiatives.

Integration and Alignment—Using Success in Cost Management to Advance toward a Truly Strategic Role for Procurement

The proverbial seat at the executive table? The heads of top-performing procurement organizations have been there for years. They talk business all the time, and they are entirely familiar with the overall company strategy.

Among procurement leaders, the CPO is twice as likely to report to the CEO and to be a member of the top management team as is the case at the average performers. These CPOs had the highest possible exposure to the company's most important business decisions; they are perfectly placed to enable swift cross-functional collaboration with peers, demonstrate procurement's position as a strategic role rather than a support function, and ensure that procurement projects have the right support from senior management. After all, they do "own" 60 to 80 percent of the productivity opportunity of the company. Of course, it takes time to get to this position, and it should go without saying that achieving the position does not happen without sustained, demonstrable performance. The CPO of a manufactured-goods company put it this way: "Only after we had spent three years delivering undisputed cost improvements of triple-digit millions to impress the board did they start taking us seriously in other areas. Now, we play a vital role in supporting product development, marketing, and manufacturing, too."

The top-performing companies in our GPE research also excel at aligning procurement strategy with the business strategy. As the procurement function becomes more sophisticated, it evolves from playing a defensive role (for instance, supporting cost control) to actively contributing to value creation. The research results show that 92 percent of leaders managed this close alignment with company strategy compared with only 67 percent of average performers and 27 percent of followers.

Practical Tips for Improving Category Management Performance

What if your organization is not performing as well as you would like with respect to the four basic dimensions of procurement excellence? What if the first change-management effort you have to undertake is to reach sophistication in classical category management? Here are some practical tips on how to build an effective category-management engine that can form the foundation for your procurement organization's enhanced value creation. With the impact of sophisticated category management providing the tailwinds, your overall transformation toward Procurement 20/20 will gain the support it needs from both management and the wider organization to pursue the much larger vision.

Every successful category-management improvement program comprises three key elements—cross-functional teams and governance, a stringent modular category management approach, and rigid performance management—all embedded in a proper communication and change plan.

Cross-Functional Category Team and Steering Governance

Successful category programs follow a total-cost approach rather than focusing solely on price. To do this, a program must involve cross-functional category teams comprising, for example, procurement, engineering, and finance. Ideally, these teams are collocated in a "war room" for at least 50 percent of the time for three to four months, and, during this period, they focus solely on generating ideas for cost reduction and execution. To develop these savings ideas, teams should use the entire procurement toolbox—for example, spend and price variance analyses, clean sheets, delta costing, tail analyses, linear performance pricing, best of benchmarking, life cycle and target costing, and specification and service-level definition. They should also conduct cross-site benchmarking and include suppliers in the idea-generation process, as appropriate.

Category teams should present and get sign-off on their comprehensive category strategies from a strategic sourcing council. Frequent steering meetings enable fast decision making, ensure that difficult topics are escalated and resolved, and identify necessary cross-functional paradigm shifts, such as an earlier involvement of procurement in the development process and tightening the supplier performance-management system.

Rigorous and Modular Category Management Approach

Successful programs start with an up-front definition of an ambitious yet realistic savings target. The target should be linked to a larger program or business need to create a sense of urgency and momentum, but it should also be broken down into teams, products, and divisions. Procurement and cross-functional partners need to share the same target. Establishing a rigid approach to category strategy development—one that entails mandatory sourcing analyses, templates, and frequent cross-functional problem solving—helps guide the teams toward their targets in a consistent way. The approach should also balance quick wins with sustainable impact.

Performance Management

Category teams require continuous tracking of results, a savings ramp-up curve, and standardized definitions of idea maturity levels to ensure progress that becomes visible on a granular level. A tracking tool should contain all savings ideas with their associated maturity level, measuring idea implementation against the savings target and simulating the savings ramp-up across all categories over time. The program management team should also develop a set of standard reports—ideally, generated automatically by the tracking tool—that communicate the progress to leaders and team members, creating a positive competitive spirit among the teams.

Any category transformation requires contributions from various stakeholders in procurement and internal customers such as finance, engineering, and legal. Consequently, every category transformation requires consistent communication and embedding of the program into a broader change plan.

■   ■   ■

Now that we have discussed what the key dimensions of a world-class procurement organization look like today, you may be wondering how you should advance your organization so that it will still be a leader in the future. What are the major trends that will affect businesses over the next decade, and how will they affect the procurement function? How should you prepare?

CHAPTER 2

The Megatrends That Impact Competitive Advantage

A procurement organization that excels across all four of the dimensions of excellence described in the previous chapter is already creating significant value for its company. But simply being prepared for today's requirements isn't good enough.

The business environment is changing faster than ever and will become more uncertain in many dimensions. The increased volatility has created a greater need for close management. In many cases, such volatility means that new conditions are superseded before some companies have even had time to react. One thing is certain, though: During the next decade, procurement will play a key role in helping companies cope with the new challenges and opportunities of this increasingly dynamic global economy. What are the major changes to expect in the decade ahead? What questions should CPOs and other company leaders be thinking about to prepare for these changes?

Consider this: Twenty years ago, China had barely entered the global economy. The world's policy forum was the G-7. The World Wide Web hardly existed. Two decades and one historic financial meltdown later, China entered the second decade of the new century as the world's second-largest economy. Policy is now being made—or at least considered—in an expanded forum, the G-20. One and a half billion people are now online, and nearly four billion have cell phones that tie them to an ever-expanding global communications grid.

The forces driving the emergence of this new world—juggernaut population trends in emerging economies; truly global markets for goods, services, labor, and capital; and unceasing innovation in fields ranging from cell phones to cell biology—are too powerful to be denied. The scale and ferocity of the recent financial crisis were amplified because of the extraordinary pace of the global integration that preceded it. Still, its most lasting effect will be to further reinforce those trends. That emerging economies led the recovery should have surprised no one. Yet it did.

McKinsey has always invested significant resources into studying the business environment. The McKinsey Global Institute (MGI), which has been at the forefront of this research, has identified five megatrends that are shaping the new global economy. These trends will have a profound effect on how CEOs, CPOs, and, in fact, all senior company leaders will lead their organizations during the next decade. From increasing an organization's capability to analyze large swaths of data to improving agility at managing increased business disruptions from natural disasters and incorporating emerging economies for value creation beyond low-cost supply and production, one thing is clear: The traditional management approaches will have to yield to a global, more integrated, more entrepreneurial, and talent-based approach. To understand what procurement organizations must do to help their company stay ahead of the competition, leaders must first understand what the world will look like in the next decade.

Megatrend 1: The Great Global Rebalancing

The vibrancy of emerging-market growth may prove to be the most profound disruption reshaping the global economy in the next decade. The next decade marks the tipping point in a fundamental, long-term economic rebalancing that will likely leave traditional Western economies with a lower share of GDP in 2050 than they had in 1700. In July 2011, General Electric (GE) announced that it planned to transition the headquarters of its 115-year-old global medical X-ray business to Beijing,[1] following second-quarter sales growth in China of 32 percent and whopping 91 percent sales growth in India, while growth expectations for developed markets were flat. Successful companies will embrace the new opportunities that arise from this Great Global Rebalancing in the form of talent, innovation, and new business models.

Private Consumption in Emerging Economies Will Grow, but Capturing the Opportunities Will Require Cost Innovation

The Great Global Rebalancing will force major adjustments in strategic focus, as emerging economies will increasingly become centers of

[1]Terril Yue Jones, Scott Malone, Jacqueline Wong, and Matthew Lewis, "GE Moving Top Executives to China," *Thomson Reuters*, July 25, 2011; "GE Looks to Low-Cost Solutions for Emerging Markets," *Trefis*, last accessed July 3, 2013, www.trefis.com/stock/ge/articles/106396/ge-healthcare-looks-to-low-cost-solutions-for-emerging-markets/2012-03-05.

consumption as well as production. More than 50 percent of the world's real gross domestic product (GDP) growth is expected to come from non–Organization for Economic Cooperation and Development (OECD) countries from 2008 through 2023, compared with only 36 percent during the previous 15 years. Virtually all major emerging markets are undergoing demographic shifts, well proven to unleash an economic miracle: More workers plus fewer mouths to feed equals more disposable income. By the end of the decade, roughly 40 percent of the world's population will have achieved middle-class status, by global standards—up from less than 20 percent today. Private consumption in emerging economies will grow to $8 trillion, or 50 percent of the world's consumption growth, by 2020, making those consumers more attractive than ever. Procter & Gamble, for example, hopes to add one billion new customers to the nearly four billion it touches today. But with only 15 percent of the purchasing power of their developed-world counterparts, these consumers still demand sophisticated country-adjusted products at a significantly lower price point.

Emerging Markets Are Becoming Sources of Innovation and Talent

The Great Global Rebalancing isn't simply a story of increasing consumption. Emerging markets will also be the world's next fount of innovation.

Companies that can innovate to reduce cost structures to 20 or 30 percent of developed-world levels can unlock a tidal wave of unmet demand. GE developed an electrocardiograph for sale in India that could be sold profitably at just 15 percent of the developed world's price point. The company built upon this effort to create a lower-cost monitor to sell in the developed world as well.

Emerging economies are also becoming home to new centers of innovation, staffed by increasingly well-educated talent. The alumni population of India's renowned Indian Institutes of Technology (IIT) has exceeded 200,000, with more than 10,000 added each year. China's research and development (R&D) expenditure, as a percentage of GDP, nearly tripled from 1995 through 2008, and the number of multinational R&D organizations located in China increased almost 40 percent from 2001 through 2006. And in 2009, for the first time ever, an emerging-market company—the Chinese telecommunications equipment manufacturer Huawei—led the world in patent applications. Not a single U.S. company made the top 10.

Is Procurement Ready?

Production in emerging economies is becoming more sophisticated, consumption in these markets is increasing, more products are being customized, and innovations are being developed and are spreading across the world. In this dynamic global marketplace, procurement must play a leading role in capturing the value at stake. But is your organization ready? Ask yourself the following:

- Are we set up to continually challenge and adapt our global sourcing footprint in order to take advantage of changing "best cost" sourcing factors such as labor cost, tax incentives, and inflation rates?
- Is our local sourcing sufficiently supporting other company functions to deliver "glocalized" products that meet the increasing demands of middle-class consumers in emerging countries? How many of these products can we take back into Western markets to drive down cost?
- Do we employ the skills, market intelligence, and organizational assets required to tap into the vast innovation opportunities and capabilities offered by the emerging markets?

Megatrend 2: The Productivity Imperative

The growth equation is simple: Growth comes from increases in the amount of labor employed and advancements in an economy's productivity. And while emerging markets ride a positive growth cycle propelled by larger and younger working populations, the developed world deals with lower birth rates and graying workforces that make it difficult to maintain what economist Adam Smith called "the natural progress of opulence." In the 1970s, the United States could rely on the growth of its labor force to generate roughly $0.80 of every dollar gained in GDP. During the next decade, that ratio will roughly invert: Labor force gains will contribute less than $0.30 to each additional dollar of economic growth. The challenge is even greater in areas such as Western Europe and Japan, where no growth or a declining workforce is expected.

Functional Specialists Are Needed to Drive Productivity

Companies have increasingly turned to external functional specialists to address the productivity imperative. More than two-thirds of productivity growth comes from product and process innovation, and companies must source even core functional activities from specialists to foster this innovation. This has resulted in a growing network of partners to manage along an end-to-end value chain.

Consider computing: Companies spend, on average, 5 to 10 percent of their total revenues on IT, but estimates suggest that upwards of 70 percent of server capacity goes unused—even more at midsize and small companies as a consequence of issues with scale. Companies have moved to cloud computing (sharing computer resources remotely) with specialists so as to simultaneously raise utilization rates, slash IT costs by 20 percent or more, and focus internal resources elsewhere.

Health care is another arena in which businesses that apply functional excellence will thrive, improving outcomes while significantly reducing costs. Health care providers are partnering with telecom providers to offer services that continually monitor diabetics and cardiac patients remotely. Health insurance providers have linked up with IT service companies to provide mobile systems that track and monitor exercise patterns so that patients—and doctors—can monitor progress and reduce risk more effectively. These companies have chosen to work with partners that have deep proficiencies rather than to waste time and resources in trying to build the capabilities themselves.

Better Management Principles Drive Productivity More Than All Other Factors

The quality of management is a much better predictor of improved productivity than is the industry sector in which a company competes, the regulatory environment that constrains it, or the country where it operates, as McKinsey research conducted with the London School of Economics suggests.[2]

Good management—be it the management of internal functions or external providers—is about methods, style, and skill, not hours clocked on the job. But what does good management look like? Well-managed companies have fostered adaptability by offering more flexible working arrangements (telecommuting options, leeway to care for sick children, choice in part-time or full-time careers, job sharing for nonmanagers), greater autonomy over decision making, and better training.

Is Procurement Ready?

Considering that external functional specialists will likely be a primary source of increased productivity for your own company, how well is your procurement function set up to successfully drive productivity in your external value chain? Ask yourself the following:

---

[2]Stephen J. Dorgan, John J. Dowdy, and Thomas M. Rippin, "The Link between Management and Productivity," *McKinseyQuarterly.com*, February 2006.

- Do we have a clear idea of which parts of the company's value chain need to be executed in-house and which are better shopped from the market?
- How well do we tap our provider network for benchmarks and competitive insights to challenge internal functions, including manufacturing, logistics, and services?
- Have we identified the best-practice providers available, and do we understand how they will evolve? How are our competitors planning to leverage their scale, low cost, and skills in the near future? How well are we equipped in procurement to truly manage our providers in an integrated way, or to orchestrate the full end-to-end value chain of external partners along a common framework, ensuring effective interfaces between external providers?

Megatrend 3: Big Data and the Global Grid

The past two decades have witnessed the rise of digital networks of unimaginable density and reach. These networks have converged to form a global communications and information grid that enables real-time interactions at scale. Old lines blur within this densely woven digital fabric. Cross-border capital flows are also information flows. Just-in-time supply chains are just-in-time information chains, too. A case in point: Just one in 10 U.S. dollars in circulation today is a physical note—the kind you can hold in your hand and put in your wallet. The other nine are virtual. And the ratio of actual ownership shares to derivatives against them is 1 to 100. Companies that win in the market will lead the way in harnessing and managing the power of this increased global connectivity.

An Explosion of Information Will Lead to New Methods of Global Connectivity

The greatest globalizer is neither capital nor trade; it's information. And the IT revolution has only just begun. Global Internet traffic is projected to increase to more than 1,000 exabytes by 2015, an almost tenfold increase since 2008. In China alone, more than 150 million first-time users connected to the Internet in 2010, giving that country a digital population almost as large as the world's biggest social networking site, Facebook. A result of this increased connectivity? The growth rate of service exports from India is expected to increase by four times the global average from 2008 through 2014.

Increasingly, not just people but also inanimate objects will plug into the planet's digital nervous system. More than 35 billion objects are connected to the Internet, including sensors, routers, and cameras. More than two-thirds of new products feature some form of smart technology, which is being used in a dizzying array of ways. For example, John Deere tractors have for years used GPS guidance systems to apply fertilizers with precision to cropland; today, software can help plan the tractor's route to optimize fuel consumption, and automatic guidance systems can steer the machine. Enterprise resource planning (ERP)-like home software for farmers can accurately predict crop yields and suggest harvest dates on the basis of weather and price information downloaded from the web.

Connecting Not Just Everyone but Also Everything Opens Up Radically New Possibilities—and Risks

The most innovative businesses will be those that harness the interlocking power of these new data sources to expand their reach and cut costs, making complex business decisions faster and better. Nortura, Norway's largest food supplier, uses radio frequency identification (RFID) technology to trace chickens from the farm to the store shelf, helping to monitor optimal refrigeration temperatures throughout the supply chain. The Dutch company TomTom has created systems that can precisely diagnose traffic jams and help reroute drivers to improve traffic flows. To acquire the data, the company has established a partnership with Vodafone that allows TomTom to install into each base station proprietary equipment that monitors the flow of mobile devices and extracts traffic information that is more accurate, timely, and fine-structured than any competing source. TomTom now even sells traffic data independent of its maps and devices.

Companies such as IBM and Cisco Systems are also aggressively developing technological approaches—from social networks to videoconferencing—that tear down organizational silos and reinvent the way that far-flung employees collaborate and exchange knowledge. What's more, these approaches work: UK grocer Tesco, for example, saved up to 45 percent of the travel budgets of key departments by substituting videoconferencing for long-haul travel.

Is Procurement Ready?

The ability to use data and connectivity to develop insights and drive superior performance has become a critical source of competitive advantage. Procurement is at the center of various data flows and connections—between internal functions and, for example, external vendors, research partners, and intellectual property (IP) providers. What can this mean for procurement? Ask yourself the following:

- How can our procurement function leverage its position at the intersection of numerous big data flows to and from the outer world, applying new analytics to create additional value?
- How can procurement, utilizing this information and analytics, deliver completely new value propositions, be it for sourcing innovation, reducing corporate risk, aiding strategic planning, or driving monetization of information to generate revenues?
- Is our category management ready for a new world of big data and sophisticated analytics?

Megatrend 4: The Volatile New Normal

The tension between rapidly rising resource consumption and environmental sustainability is sure to become one of the next decade's critical pressure points. Natural resources and commodities account for roughly 10 percent of global GDP and underpin every sector of the economy. And as the earth's resources are impacted by natural disasters, fluctuate in price, or worse, run out, the reverberations will be felt across the globe. In November 2011, computer hard-drive prices almost doubled, from $0,055 to $0,095 per GB, within days.[3] Intel cut its fourth-quarter sales outlook by $1 billion. Sony, Sharp, and Panasonic announced substantial losses, and Lenovo admitted that it had incurred an additional cost of $5 to $10 for each hard drive it shipped with its computers. Why did all of these companies suffer these blows? Because in July 2011, serious floods in Thailand had badly damaged the Seagate and Western Digital production plants in the area, leaving supply short and causing prices to spike.

---

[3]Joel Hruska, "Storage Pricewatch: HDDs Back to Pre-Flood Prices, SDDs Grow as $/GB Holds Steady," *Extreme Tech*, accessed July 3, 2013, www.extremetech.com/computing/153879-storage-pricewatch-hdds-back-to-pre-flood-prices-ssds-grow-as-gb-holds-steady; "Thai Flood Impact on Tech Companies' Suppliers," *Boston Globe*, accessed July 3, 2013, www.boston.com/business/technology/articles/2012/02/22/thai_flooding_impact_on_tech_companies_suppliers/?page=3; Jose Vilches, "HDD Pricewatch: Three Months into the Thai Floods," *Techspot*, accessed July 3, 2013, www.techspot.com/guides/494-hard-drive-pricewatch-thai-floods/.

Demand for Many Natural Resources Is Outstripping Supply

Even the most conservative projections for global economic growth over the next decade suggest that demand for oil, coal, iron ore, and other natural resources will rise by at least one-third. About 90 percent of that increase will come from growth in emerging markets. Yet, easy-to-tap and high-quality reserves are nearly depleted, and supply will have to come from locations that are harder and more costly to access and, possibly, politically unstable.

World demand for energy continues to increase. While some existing projects to improve oil supply will decline in productivity at an accelerating rate, others, such as hydraulic fracturing (or "fracking"), are just becoming viable. Successful new exploration projects are increasingly rare and substantially more difficult to exploit.

Worldwide, annual food demand is forecast to rise to 12 billion metric tons by 2050, twice the level of 2005. But agricultural output has not been keeping pace: wheat output, for example, dropped from 1997 through 2007. Changing temperatures could reduce agricultural productivity, striking South Asia and sub-Saharan Africa the hardest and leading to gradual replacement of tropical forests by savannas in the eastern Amazon basin.

Water scarcity is becoming a global phenomenon, with more than 250 million people likely to be subject to severe water stress by 2020. This will affect both developed and developing economies, with select regions of the United States, European Union, and Australia already impacted, and northern China, the Middle East, Africa, and India under particular stress.

Furthermore, markets are increasingly interconnected, which has amplified volatility. Prices for oil and plastics have always been correlated, as have oil and energy prices. Now, however, alternative technologies have meant that food prices are correlated with oil prices and weather, on both the demand and the supply sides.

Commodity Prices Will Rise Higher and Fall Harder

For most resource commodities, the question is not whether supply will be sufficient but what will happen to prices. And that depends in part on what it takes to gain access to the commodities.

Just four countries—Iran, Iraq, Saudi Arabia, and Venezuela—hold some 50 percent of known oil and gas reserves. Nationally owned oil companies now control more than 85 percent of those reserves. Many of the key providers are highly exposed to geopolitical instability, making supply security a major risk. Meanwhile, new supply is proving harder to find. Most new sources—such as deep-sea reserves or oil sands—require high-priced, environmentally controversial approaches to extraction.

Adding to the complexity is the fickle nature of global commodities markets. The number of "virtual" barrels of oil, in the form of futures and derivatives, that are traded on global exchanges each day exceeds the number of real barrels by a ratio estimated at 30 to 1. This market effect, enabled by the global grid, amplifies every market tremor—a key reason for the collapse of oil prices to just 25 percent of precrisis levels in the immediate wake of the financial crisis.

Consider copper: More than half of world production is concentrated in a handful of countries (including Chile and Peru) that have limited infrastructure and high extraction costs. Demand can only grow, but producers are wary of investing in infrastructure ahead of the demand cycle—a strategy that practically guarantees future pricing volatility.

Caustic soda, a chemical used ubiquitously in the manufacture of goods, showcases a spectacular rise in prices—followed by a spectacular fall. Typically sold for less than $400 per dry short ton in the United States through 2007, it spiked to higher than $1,000 in 2008 when producers stopped making it—a result of the inability to sell chlorine, its dangerous coproduct, into the collapsing housing market. Prices then fell to less than $200 in 2009 when customers moved away in droves.

And innovation will often render materials worthless in a matter of weeks, at the same time driving the demand for new ones. In 2009, BMW and SGL Group formed a joint venture to provide the exclusive supply of carbon fiber to BMW's new models. Two years later, both BMW and Volkswagen started to take significant positions in SGL Group to secure future supply, competing for a bigger share and increased influence. The growing use of carbon fiber in structural engineering spurred not only the tripling of SGL Group's share price between 2009 and 2012 but also the skyrocketing of demand (and prices) for the material. Meanwhile, aluminum, which is being replaced by other materials, has seen significant price pressures.

Is Procurement Ready?

More than one CPO has lost his or her job for not being able to "supply the factory"—the primary objective of any procurement organization and one that, in this volatile world, is getting harder to master. Responding to the volatility simply by paying insurance premiums is not an option, and it is the defensive view. Instead, how can procurement help turn volatility and scarcity into competitive advantage? Ask yourself the following:

- How transparent are the various risks in our supply chain to us as the decision makers? Do we know which risks to examine more thoroughly, determining those that require mitigating action, and which to accept?

- How adequate are our current business-continuity plans for coping with the most virulent supply risks? Will they save the company?
- How can procurement turn better market insight and understanding of risk exposure into a competitive weapon, by reacting faster or even barring competitors from access to scarce resources?

Megatrend 5: The New Economic Drivers

While we expect the steady advance of market capitalism to continue, governments are likely to play an even larger role over the next decade. The recent financial crisis prompted governments everywhere to mitigate the negative impact on their individual citizens—by providing fiscal stimuli, shortening the balance sheet, and calling for increased regulation. And as the number of regulations increases, so do the calls by consumer and advocacy groups for increased stewardship of the environment and improved working conditions for employees. The influence of environmental, social, and regulatory (ESR) issues will be greater than ever. One common characteristic of all these interventions is that they are almost all sudden and drastic.

Global Companies Must Learn to Navigate Diverse Regulatory and Social Issues

As companies expand globally, they will need to become more sophisticated about navigating the increasingly complex regulatory landscape. The annual growth rate of China's export-tax rebate, for example, has swung wildly from as low as –40 percent to +60 percent from 1987 through 2007, changing the attractiveness of procuring goods from China in any given year. And the ban on plastic materials for use as food containers by local governments in the Philippines has cut production by 50 percent since 2010, with further reductions expected to kill the industry as other local governments jump on the bandwagon. Changes in government regulations can have a significant impact on the profitability of any industry.

And around the world, political leaders, regulators, scientific experts, and consumers are gravitating to a new consensus—one based on fostering environmental sustainability. Climate change is the most highly charged and visible battleground, but other issues loom: water scarcity, pollution, food safety, and the depletion of global fishing stocks. Tax levies are not always logical: In many cases, they are thinly disguised attempts to fill the government coffers. For businesses, this new sensibility will result in environmental regulations that differ widely from one country to another and even more divergent demands from consumers and employees that companies demonstrate greater environmental responsibility.

Managing a diverse social landscape is also difficult. Safety and labor standards will remain fragmented, varying across countries and regions. The deaths of 300 garment workers in a 2012 factory fire in Pakistan and more than 1,000 in a 2013 building collapse in Bangladesh, the result of weak regulations supporting the burgeoning textile industry, serve as a reminder that tragedy can strike at any time and that responsible audit measures must be put in place to prevent it. Still, as the global grid expands, the fallout from a single misstep in one country will ripple at the speed of light to more and more places, in new ways that will make the earlier experiences of companies—from shoe manufacturers to oil producers—seem relatively simple. Companies will need to become even more proactive and dynamic to better manage the increasing ESR demands.

Is Procurement Ready?

Addressing new standards imposed by consumers, industry, advocacy groups, and governments will be a daunting challenge, but one that procurement is well positioned to help the company meet. Quite a few CPOs have already taken on responsibility for driving the sustainability agendas of their companies. But there is more opportunity. Ask yourself the following:

- Do we understand the total ESR cost and risks of our supply? In other words, the total impact of ownership?
- How good are our sourcing decisions today, and to what extent do they already reflect full ESR costs and risks?
- How can our procurement organization help drive these costs down, making them transparent, establishing them as an important element in sourcing decision making, and even proactively supporting our lobbying efforts and efforts to build relationships with nongovernmental organizations (NGOs) and governments?
- How can we leverage advanced ESR best practices in our supply chain for the entire company's sustainability profile and positioning?

■   ■   ■

Although we have extracted some of the implications explicitly for procurement, you undoubtedly recognize that these megatrends will touch every function of your organization: Sales will need to improve the company's connectedness with the consumers of the emerging world, launching products that are tailored specifically for them; R&D must turn into a flexible engine of design to deliver products that can make use of a variety of inputs in the face of material or cost volatility; and external relations must understand the voice of the social activist, the government, and environmental groups, swiftly identifying, prioritizing, and reducing risks associated with ESR. We strongly believe that procurement has a tremendous opportunity to undertake a mission of "supply entrepreneurship" and add more value in this new and dynamic global economy. The questions at the end of each trend should have triggered some thinking already.

In the next part, "Responding to the Megatrends of the Next Decade," we take a closer look at each of these megatrends, consider the possibilities for how procurement can lead the effort to capture value, and discuss the capabilities that procurement organizations must build to step up to their new and expanded role.

PART 2

Responding to the Megatrends of the Next Decade

CHAPTER 3

The Great Global Rebalancing: Building a Dynamic Sourcing Footprint

Main Messages

- Sourcing will take place across the entire world; "white spaces" that may exist today will disappear. The future of the sourcing organization therefore is global and multicultural.
- Sourcing-footprint considerations will become increasingly multidimensional and dynamic. Sourcing decisions will have to be made against the backdrop of an integrated company footprint, including manufacturing, sales, and R&D.
- Procurement is in a prime position to lead these integrated company-footprint considerations given its deep cross-functional nature and thorough understanding of global and local markets.

For many Western manufacturers, the question of where to source once had a simple answer: China. The primary driver was lowering the cost of the supplied goods. The days when a company could use product cost as the principal factor in defining a sourcing footprint are long gone, however. Over the past decade, additional factors—including logistics, currency, lead time, and export and import duties—have become more important than ever, meaning that product cost, though still a primary factor, is no longer the principal factor.

Consider the European furniture retailer Ikea, which has a sales and sourcing footprint in Asia and plans to enter the Indonesian market. Several questions arise for the chief procurement officer (CPO). From which region should the company source merchandise for the products it sells in Indonesia? Should it establish new sourcing relationships with local suppliers in Indonesia to gain the benefit of proximity to its retail locations and better meet local product needs? Are there local regulatory issues to consider? Should it rely instead on its established supply base (China and Vietnam) for the region? What role should the company's own factories in Eastern Europe and India play in serving the new stores? For each option, what are the key supply chain characteristics, and how might these characteristics affect the sourcing cost drivers?

In the future, an even broader set of factors will determine sourcing decisions. Companies will have to consider, among other factors, the emergence of developing countries as new sales markets, access to talent, localization of production, and risk, environmental, social, and regulatory issues. As a result, a sourcing footprint will become more dynamic—and so will the process for defining it. Decisions that require complex trade-offs among a wide range of objectives and motivations will have to be made. This greater complexity stems from the Great Global Rebalancing of the global economy that will continue to redefine how companies pursue a competitive advantage in the coming decade. The term refers to a rebalancing of global economic activity from Europe and North America to Asia, South America, and Africa.

Most companies recognize that new forces are at work and have begun to make sourcing decisions based on this wider range of indirect and overlapping cost factors. But few companies react dynamically to redefine their optimal sourcing footprint, which is constantly influenced by the factors cited previously, so that they can capture the full range of opportunities with respect to costs and capabilities. To remedy that shortcoming, companies can begin by recognizing that the procurement organization is naturally positioned to lead the effort to develop and manage a dynamic sourcing footprint, one that is optimally integrated with the overall corporate footprint, which includes sales, product development, and manufacturing, among other functions.

The growing complexity of input factors for decisions will require companies to consider multiple variables in optimizing the available sourcing-footprint scenarios, obtain a truly global view of the supply base, and tightly integrate strategic and operational thinking and planning among a company's functions.

Dynamic Sourcing in a Rebalanced World

During the past 20 years, two dynamic and overarching factors have shaped the Great Global Rebalancing: the growth of emerging markets and the economic slowdown in developed markets.

Emerging markets' growth has been fueled by the increasing size and urbanization of the consumer class. In 2025, the consumer class globally will number 4.2 billion. Consumption in emerging markets will account for U.S. $30 trillion—nearly half of the global total[1] (see Exhibit 3.1). It is fair to assume that, in a reasonable economic equilibrium, consumption will be equal to production in value; thus, emerging markets will also be the sourcing ground of the future.

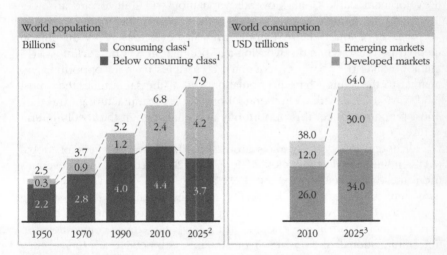

EXHIBIT 3.1 World Population versus World Consumption. In 2025, the consuming class will have reached 4.2 billion. Consumption in emerging markets will account for U.S. $30 trillion—nearly half the global total.

[1]Consuming class—daily disposable income is ≥USD10; below consuming class, <USD10; incomes adjusted for purchasing-power parity.
[2]Projected.
[3]Estimate based on 2010 private-consumption share of GDP per country and GDP estimates for 2010 and 2025; assumes private consumption's share of GDP will remain constant.
Source: Angus Maddison, founder of the Groningen Growth and Development Centre, University of Groningen; Homi Kharas, senior fellow at the Wolfensohn Center for Development at the Brookings Institution; McKinsey Global Institute analysis.

---

[1]Yuval Atsmon, Peter Child, Richard Dobbs, and Laxman Narasimhan, "Winning the $30 Trillion Decathlon: Going for Gold in Emerging Markets," *McKinseyQuarterly.com*, August 2012.

At the same time, the economic growth in developed markets has not kept pace with that of emerging markets. In many developed countries, growth has stagnated as a series of crises have taken their toll, from Japan's "lost decade" to the Great Recession and the European debt crisis.

As a result, GDP growth has shifted significantly in favor of emerging markets. During the next 10 to 15 years, these two factors—the rise of emerging markets and the stagnation of developed markets—will have an even more pervasive impact.

What does the Great Global Rebalancing look like at a granular level? Consider China, which has emerged as both an abundant source of supply and a major source of consumer demand. According to the Asian Development Bank, China's overall population will shift toward an older demographic more quickly than any other country, beginning in 2015.[2] As of 2020, China's elderly population will be increasing by 10 million people per year, while the working-age population will be declining by 7 million adults per year. Consequently, companies have an opportunity to market to the aging Chinese population. But at the same time, they must find ways to deal with a shrinking labor pool for manufacturing. And they must prepare to meet this opportunity and challenge in the medium-term future.

Although emerging markets are responsible for 46 percent of global GDP, multinational companies capture only 20 percent of their revenues from these markets (see Exhibit 3.2).[3] During the next 10 years, the procurement functions of multinational companies will have a lot of catching up to do. They now face more and more competition from local companies in emerging markets; often, in just a few years, those companies turn into multinationals themselves. To maintain a competitive advantage, they must leverage their market knowledge, lower-cost operating models, and existing supplier base.

To respond effectively to the opportunities and challenges created by the Great Global Rebalancing, most multinational companies are moving strongly into emerging markets as a new supplier base, as well as a manufacturing hub. They often apply this experience to establish local sales activities and, eventually, even product development activities.

---

[2]Yolanda Fernandez Lommen, "The Socioeconomic Implications of Population Aging in the People's Republic of China," *ADB Briefs*, October 2010, accessed February 20, 2013, www2.adb.org/documents/briefs/ADB-Briefs-2010-6-Population-Aging-PRC.pdf.
[3]Atsmon, Child, Dobbs, and Narasimhan, "Winning the $30 Trillion Decathlon."

Markets' contribution to global GDP versus leading global companies' share of total revenues[1] from given markets, 2011, percent

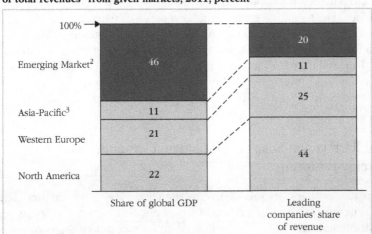

EXHIBIT 3.2 Share of Global GDP versus Leading Companies' Share of Revenue. Leading companies in the developed world earn just 20 percent of total revenues from emerging markets, even though these markets represent 46 percent of global GDP.

[1]For 100 of the world's largest companies headquartered in developed economies, excluding oil and gas companies.
[2]Asia-Pacific, Latin America, Eastern Europe, Middle East/Africa.
[3]Asia-Pacific (developed) includes Australia, Japan, New Zealand, Singapore, South Korea, Hong Kong, and Taiwan.
Source: Company financials; McKinsey analysis.

By developing their footprint across a range of functions in emerging markets, multinational companies can generate savings of up to 25 percent. Beyond lower costs, emerging markets also offer improved skills and capabilities, as evidenced by their increased production and export of high-tech products. New talent pools can also be found throughout the world. For example, African countries, led by South Africa, have become locations where European companies outsource information technology (IT) and business process tasks.[4]

---

[4]Imara Africa Securities Team, "Why Outsourcing Could Be Africa's Next Big Opportunity," www.howwemadeitinafrica.com/why-outsourcing-could-be-africas-next-big-opportunity/9793/.

What does the rise of emerging markets mean for procurement? In a world subject to continued rebalancing, the sourcing footprint itself must be able to adapt so that the company can maintain a competitive advantage in the rapidly changing global market landscape. The sourcing footprint must become fully interlinked with the footprints of other company functions, such as manufacturing, sales, and R&D. And it needs to be adaptable so as to take advantage of cost, revenue, and innovation opportunities appearing in the global marketplace.

What Factors Will Shape the Global and Dynamic Sourcing Footprint?

Given the evolving nature of the rebalancing world, the factors shaping the sourcing footprint are changing as well. Still, seven factors are playing an increasingly important role in shaping a company's global sourcing footprint:

1. Sourcing at best cost
2. Serving local customers
3. Providing anchor points for the overall company footprint
4. Capturing the advantages of innovation and related capabilities
5. Mitigating supply chain risks
6. Addressing sustainability issues
7. Responding to government regulations

Sourcing at Best Cost

For many years, China was the go-to destination for Western companies seeking low-cost supply. But ultralow costs in some countries are enabling companies to pursue a wider range of options. Best-cost sourcing entails exploring alternatives in Asian countries other than China; the situation is similar in Africa, Eastern Europe, and Latin America. The objective is to achieve a total cost advantage by tapping into low-cost manufacturing and the best logistics costs. In manufacturing, Vietnam, Indonesia, and Bangladesh are part of a "China plus one" strategy for low-cost country sourcing. For example, a large contract manufacturer of electronics plans to build its second-largest assembly plant in Indonesia. Another electronics contract manufacturer plans to invest more than $100 million to build plants in Vietnam to produce touch screens. This strategy is also being applied in Latin America, where automotive suppliers have used Honduras and Nicaragua as best-cost sourcing alternatives to Mexico. And South

Africa has been developing low-cost manufacturing capabilities, as demonstrated by German and U.S. automakers' agreements to outsource parts from suppliers in that country.

However, the gravity of sourcing is not shifting entirely to developing countries. Another factor is influencing cost-based sourcing decisions (although many companies have not yet focused sufficiently on it): Unfavorable economic conditions in developed countries have shifted bargaining power from employees to employers. Manufacturing employees and unions (and government officials who oversee the labor force) are more willing to accept reduced salaries in exchange for job creation. While labor costs in China have soared over the past decade (salaries have increased by 180 percent on China's east coast), high levels of unemployment have led to flat or declining wage levels in some developed countries—for example, in the United States, the annual growth rate of wages has fallen to 2 percent since the beginning of the recession, from 20 percent in the preceding four years.

For U.S. companies, these factors have combined to make "reshoring" a viable option. For example, Ford has shifted 1,500 jobs from Mexico, China, and Japan to plants in Ohio, Michigan, and Missouri; General Electric decided to put U.S. $1 billion into the group's domestic appliances business to create hundreds of jobs in Louisville, Kentucky; and even Lenovo, the Chinese manufacturer that took over the PC business from IBM, has started a new PC production line in Whitsett, North Carolina. Such reshoring is also motivated by other factors: the desire to protect intellectual property, increases in U.S. import tariffs for some goods, tax incentives, the benefits of flexibly responding to demand fluctuations, and lower logistics costs.[5]

Serving Local Customers

To match the success of local champions in emerging markets, leading multinational companies have recognized that they must manufacture and sell products tailored to local needs. Their current global products may be either poorly suited to meeting local needs or insufficient by themselves to attract consumers. To achieve the objective of "going local," companies "glocalize" their products by locally adapting, producing, and sourcing products for a specific country. For example, Frito-Lay has introduced a

---

[5]"Here, There, and Everywhere," Special Report Outsourcing and Offshoring, *Economist*, January 13, 2013, and Ed Crooks, "GE Takes $1bn Risk in Bringing Jobs Home," *Financial Times*, April 2, 2012.

variety of glocalized products, such as chips flavored with chili or seaweed for the Thai consumer market; soy sauce, octopus, or bento beef flavor for Japan; and "Kurkure," a snack flavored with masala, green chutney, and tamatar, for India.

Unilever is using the same glocalization strategy in Indonesia. In 2011, one-third of Unilever's revenues in the country came from products costing 20 cents or less. For example, the company introduced a single-use shampoo sachet to sell to rural consumers who cannot afford the standard-sized shampoo bottle or lack storage space for personal-care products. Unilever has created a local supply base to enable the production of these goods.[6]

Providing Anchor Points for the Overall Company Footprint

In sourcing from a developing country over a period of years, companies typically acquire significant experience about the country's supply base, supply chain costs, market dynamics, regulations, and more. Local procurement professionals build relationships with local companies, authorities, regulators, and communities. Both the local experience and the relationships can greatly help a company advance the footprints of its other functions in a country or region.

For example, Carrefour leveraged its existing procurement organization in China to launch new stores. The retailer established sourcing operations in China in 1993 and opened its first hypermarket in the country two years later. Its relationships with local officials allowed it to fast-track central government approval for new stores, while its existing local presence allowed it to quickly understand and adapt to local needs. Its stores are supplied locally and managed as profit centers. In 2010, the retailer had 203 hypermarkets in 60 Chinese cities, and €5.7 billion in annual revenues from China and Taiwan.

In other industries, the link between a company's sourcing footprint and its manufacturing or sales footprint is even more clear. Consider governments' localization requirements that automotive original equipment manufacturers (OEMs) are facing in many developing countries when they want to build up local manufacturing subsidiaries. Or consider the industrial offset requirements that Japan imposed on Boeing as a condition to selling aircraft to Japanese carriers: To gain preferred market access, Boeing sourced fuselage sections for the 767 and many other parts for other aircraft types from Japanese subcontractors.

---

[6]"Fighting for the Next Billion Shoppers," *Economist*, June 30, 2012, and "Hanging Tough in Indonesia," *Bloomberg Businessweek*, April 1, 2002.

In both cases, the sourcing footprint proved to be an important anchor point that would allow other functions to expand their operations in the country.

Capturing the Advantages of Innovation and Related Capabilities

Developing countries are more than growth markets for products. They have enhanced their sourcing and technological capabilities for innovation, becoming creators of products as well as sources of supply. Until recently, companies in emerging markets were not known for their innovation strengths, but in the past five years the number of patent applications from companies in emerging markets has increased significantly. China has surpassed the European Union and South Korea in patent applications filed since 2007 and now ranks second only to the United States on that measure. ZTE, a Chinese multinational telecommunications company, and Huawei ranked first and third, respectively, in terms of patent applications in 2011. What's more, the number of patent applications from China relating to inventions has grown in recent years to match the number related to new ideas applied to existing products. Quality standards are also reaching world-class levels, as evidenced by the increase in Chinese exports of radiology and ultrasound equipment during the past five years. India, on the other hand, continues to be the hotbed of standard IT development, providing the world's workbench for these developments.

Several multinational companies have built R&D facilities in emerging markets—and not only in China or India. For example, Nokia Siemens Network has opened an R&D facility in the Philippines. And new or "reverse" innovations created in developing countries are influencing the market. For example, more than 20 million people in Africa use a mobile wallet developed in African countries, including Kenya, Nigeria, and Ghana.

Closer to the West, emerging markets in Central and Eastern Europe, Mexico, and Latin America also offer advanced capabilities and well-educated workers. Recognizing that advanced capabilities are available at lower cost, many companies are sourcing pools of highly educated people in emerging markets.

Mitigating Supply Chain Risks

Managing the risks of a diverse supply chain has become more complex. Many companies that have made forays into global sourcing have experienced unexpected costs stemming from a variety of situations: natural disasters, disease outbreaks among livestock, and economic or political crises. A wide range of industries has been affected, from agriculture to automotive and electronics. For example, the electronics industry was heavily affected when a flooding disaster occurred in Thailand in 2011, causing a major disruption in PC production and creating the need for significant price increases. Similarly, restrictions imposed by the Chinese government on access to rare earths in 2010 caused prices to skyrocket and led some electronics companies to stockpile supplies of these minerals. This governmental action also led to the resumption of mining activities outside of China. CPOs are well advised to take supply chain risk considerations into account when designing their overall sourcing footprint. We will discuss the strategies to deal with enhanced supply chain risks in more detail in Chapter 6.

Addressing Sustainability Issues

Global sourcing has exposed companies to a greater number of environmental and ethical issues (which we will consider further in Chapter 7). Exposure to these issues has grown, as has consumer awareness and interest. Sales of "green" and ethical products are increasing, and consumers have become more aware of related issues that arise in companies' global supply chains. The ethical treatment of suppliers' employees and area residents has become a prominent concern that CPOs will have to deal with.

Responding to Government Regulations

Many governments have raised import tariffs and local content requirements to protect local industries and encourage multinational companies to invest in developing the local supply base.

CPOs must make an effort to maintain acceptable costs in response to import taxes and local content requirements. For example, as part of its industrial policy in 2011, Brazil announced a new import tax that would affect clothing, footwear, and automotive industries, among others. In response, several automotive companies that had not previously established production lines in Brazil announced investments in the country so that their production footprint and local supply base would allow them to remain competitive. Similarly, high import tariffs have led OEMs to set up plants in India to produce vehicles for low-cost segments, complementing the need for low-cost production to serve these consumers.

Governments influence companies' sourcing footprints through tariffs but also as buyers. With increasing spend in infrastructure as well as wealth generated from natural resources, governments ask for local content in exchange for business. This will require companies to design carefully the activities they pursue in a new market.

The evolving nature of regulations promoting localization makes it critical for companies to develop a dynamic response and to consider long-term impact. Significant investments are required for compliance, but the regulations themselves are subject to change. For example, to encourage automotive OEMs and suppliers to increase local production levels, Russia had implemented both an import tax and local content requirements. In connection with its accession to the World Trade Organization (WTO) in 2012, however, Russia needed to reduce its import tariffs. To maintain incentives for local production, the country has imposed a recycling fee on vehicles that includes an exemption for those produced in a special economic zone. In Brazil, setting up operations or a supply base in a particular state can confer tax advantages that can amount to 25 percent of total costs. But there is no guarantee that such tax advantages will continue indefinitely, especially considering that the Brazilian government has announced its intention to end the tax war between states in order to attract industry. In the absence of tax benefits, other factors—higher logistics costs, for example—could make local operations financially unfeasible.

All these factors are not only driving decisions on the right sourcing footprint, but also constantly changing in weight, direction, and priority. As a natural consequence, sourcing decision making and sourcing footprints must also become much more *dynamic* in the future. This is the new normal with regard to the Great Global Rebalancing that CPOs must be prepared to cope with.

Dynamic Sourcing in Action: Two Case Examples

As CPOs think about how a dynamic sourcing footprint might evolve to address the complexity of a rebalanced world in the decade ahead, two case examples relating to government tariffs help illustrate the possibilities:

Indonesia imposed an export tariff on metal ore to encourage companies to invest in processing facilities in the country.[7] Indonesia is the largest supplier of nickel and bauxite for Chinese manufacturers, which means that the new tariff will have a significant impact. How might CPOs respond? Options may include shifting supply to

---

[7]"Indonesia Imposes New Taxes on Metal Exports," *New York Times*, May 4, 2012.

other countries, such as the Philippines, Russia, or Canada; aligning with manufacturing and logistics to build or buy a smelter plant in the country; exploring suitable alternative raw materials, such as copper-based composites; or even working with the company's legal department to investigate WTO compliance issues and seek to negotiate an exemption.

India and France announced plans in 2012 to increase palm oil import tariffs by up to an additional 300 percent.[8] India raised the import tariff to increase the competitiveness of local palm oil refineries after palm oil imports from Indonesia more than doubled within one year following a reduction in that country's export tariff. A cosmetics manufacturer with Indian plants that imports palm oil from Indonesia should reevaluate where to source palm oil based on total costs. Building a palm oil refinery in India might be an option if the total cost is lower than maintaining a refinery in Indonesia or another country such as Malaysia. In addition, CPOs should consider alternative raw materials—such as coconut, rapeseed, or sunflower oil. Because these alternatives may also enable the company to promote "greener" products, the CPO should work with marketing to consider the branding benefits.

Capabilities for Defining a Dynamic Footprint

The optimal dynamic sourcing footprint can be determined only in concert with other company functions, such as R&D, sales, and manufacturing. The sourcing footprint will be the result of an optimization of the respective footprints of these functions. As a consequence, not only is it determined by multiple, dynamic drivers, but it also needs to be more adaptable—changing supply locations has to be much easier than entering a new country or setting up factories. Supplier relationship and development activities, accelerated learning curves, long-term contracts—all of these are likely to become more relevant. What's more, given that factors affecting the sourcing footprint are the most dynamic, CPOs are likely to be the first functional leaders to have visibility into how conditions are changing, and the first to possess a fact base that can be used to inform footprint decisions. They must lead and own the change and thus become supply

---

[8]"Govt Raises Tariff Value of Refined Palm Oil to USD 1,053/ton," *Economic Times*, August 1, 2012.

entrepreneurs. Consequently, procurement is well positioned to act as the convener of issues that other functions must discuss to determine the company's overall footprint as well as the respective functional footprints. To step up to this role, CPOs must develop three primary capabilities. First, they need to build convening power to drive integrated footprint decisions. For that, they need to establish a global, cross-functional fact base. And with these two in place, they can start building the skills to design and implement flexible supply chains.

Build Convening Power to Drive Integrated Footprint Decisions across Functions

To build a mandate for the convener's role and fulfill it effectively, CPOs must develop close ties with their peers in other functions, such as manufacturing and sales. They must demonstrate that they have the relevant market insights and understand the implications for the functional footprints. It will be critical to stay a step ahead of peers on footprint issues and to proactively make suggestions regarding how to adapt footprints in response to the dynamic environment and how to challenge the status quo. CPOs can also use the sourcing relationships they develop in new markets as bridgeheads that other functions can leverage to expand their own footprints, or to tap into innovations in the local supply base.

For example, CPOs must generate insights into how factors such as the development of a supply base, the fluctuations of currency, and the changes to export and import tariffs affect the cost advantages of establishing a manufacturing footprint in a particular country. In defining a footprint to implement glocalization, procurement must work with marketing and sales to analyze data on local consumer preferences and competition. Footprint decisions regarding best-cost sourcing may require a careful assessment of government incentives and strategy, such as the tax exemptions available in some regions to encourage job creation. These assessments require collaborating with the legal department to understand not only the current tax advantages but also the likelihood that they will be maintained going forward.

To make this collaboration happen, procurement organizations should establish and facilitate regular interactions among the functional stakeholders to holistically discuss the company's integrated footprint development and the related challenges. To be effective, they should include "footprint forums," interactive strategy sessions, scenario plays, and the extensive use of classical management frameworks—structure-conduct-performance (SCP), Porter's five forces, and others. In addition to these senior alignment sessions, procurement should deploy people close to the respective markets and functions in order to be well informed. One of the world's leading food companies provides an example. The procurement function established a group of buyers with backgrounds in R&D, and assigned them to business units specifically to serve as links between procurement and these units' new market opportunities and needs. At the end of the first year of the new organization and operating model, the time to market for new-product development had been reduced from 14 to 9 months.

Establish a Global, Cross-Functional Fact Base to Support Footprint Decision Making

CPOs will find it easier to convene senior functional leaders to discuss and adapt the company's footprint amid environmental changes if they bring clear value to the table. The procurement function's most valuable contribution to these discussions will be superior insights. From an internal perspective, procurement must thoroughly understand other functions' footprint requirements and drivers, including market entry strategies and manufacturing insourcing or outsourcing strategies. Procurement is also in a good position to leverage its existing network of relationships in different markets to provide an external fact base to support holistic footprint decisions. The information collected and provided should extend beyond sourcing issues to cover overall country information, local business development, and operational insights.

To gain a cross-functional perspective on overall footprint opportunities, procurement can gather insights on national and regional economic development, such as with respect to currency and wages. It can understand how a market is changing, covering issues such as the evolution of supply and demand, demographics, and regulations. Knowing the strengths and weaknesses of the country's infrastructure is another insight that procurement can naturally pick up from being close to the respective market; assessing risks stemming from national or regional incidents or tensions will be a similar vantage point.

Sourcing can also easily generate insights into the local business environment that are specifically valuable to business development, marketing, and sales. These insights include market-segment growth rates or competitor moves and behaviors that can, for example, be tapped by talking to suppliers. Procurement could go so far as to try to reconstruct a competitor's manufacturing footprint, supply base, technological maturity, and supply chain model from these insights, thereby greatly helping business development define its own market entry and footprint strategy.

Similarly, procurement can naturally gather insights relevant to the manufacturing function in defining its footprint. This includes the development of labor costs and skills, structural costs (such as real estate, rents, and utilities), tax incentives, and the best regions for locating factories. It can also understand the competitive manufacturing landscape, as well as identify local companies that offer opportunities for outsourcing, partnerships, or serving as suppliers.

Sourcing would also naturally collect insights specific to defining the appropriate sourcing footprint: classic supply base information, the extent to which local suppliers would need to develop capabilities to achieve the company's standards, supplier cost models, suppliers' capabilities to provide innovations that meet local needs, and so on.

Ultimately, procurement could strive to build the total, cross-functional fact base needed to inform corporate-level footprint decisions. This fact base is largely a natural extension of the fact base that category managers already assemble during the course of their sourcing work. Even so, extending the fact base will require category managers (who are often heavily involved and immersed in daily supply issues) to obtain a much broader view of the business. Deep knowledge of sophisticated total cost of ownership (TCO) models will be critical for understanding glocalization, reshoring, best-cost sourcing, and other strategies relevant to cross-functional footprint planning.

Design and Implement Flexible Supply Chains to Operationalize the Global Footprint

Once a new sourcing footprint is defined to complement the overall company footprint and plan, it must be translated into individual, flexible supply chains that deliver the goods and services required. Flexible supply chains are able to respond proactively to the world's dynamically changing environment, thereby enabling the company to optimize costs and produce more competitive goods and services. Flexibility manifests itself in the availability of more active and passive supply options.

Consider the example of Zara, the Spain-based fast-fashion company. To encourage consumers to visit stores more often and to buy more when they do, Zara has introduced three to six times more items each year than its competitors and shortened the lead time required to reflect consumers' changing tastes in its products. Zara's lead time for new products from design to store shelves is four to five weeks, in contrast to eight weeks or more for competitors. It modifies existing product lines within two weeks.

To enable this rapid response, Zara applies different supply chain and manufacturing footprint strategies. For fast fashion, Zara takes advantage of nearshoring opportunities by integrating its supply chain and manufacturing footprints close to its store locations. Zara outsources sewing to hundreds of workshops in Galicia and northern Portugal. Its vertical manufacturing is located primarily in Spain. Fashion design R&D is also located in Spain, so it can connect directly to fashion shows and on-the-street research. The input from the market research goes straight to the designers, and the material needs for the new products are rapidly communicated to suppliers. For products outside its fast-fashion line, Zara has started to outsource from Asia. Because these products are less sensitive to seasonal change and have classic form, the company can take advantage of low-cost production and longer lead times.

When designing their footprints, other industries also take advantage of nearshoring to accommodate short lead times. For example, automotive manufacturers outsource their wiring from nearshore locations to gain the flexibility needed for just-in-time (JIT) supply for production and the actual development and face-lifts of the design. Ford outsourced its wiring to Flextronics in Mexico to be fairly close to Ford's production and development facilities in Detroit, in the same way as Smarteq, supplier of antennas to Volkswagen, bases its assembly line in Eastern Europe at significantly lower labor cost.

■ ■ ■

Four aspirations should guide CPOs as they seek to lead their procurement organizations to achieve these objectives in a rebalanced world. Procurement must seek to become:

- A local player and the company's source of deep expertise with respect to the cultural, legal, and political attributes of the global marketplace.
- The front-runner in the company's move into new markets, helping prepare the ground for other functions.
- The convener among different functions' global footprint considerations, and the analytical thought leader behind the company's integrated global footprint.
- The proponent of flexible supply chains that can adapt to the ongoing changes brought about by the Great Global Rebalancing.

The rebalancing of economic power toward developing countries puts a challenge to Western economies: How can they maintain wealth creation through productivity gains and innovation? To address this challenge, many companies are turning to best-practice functional specialists to perform an ever-increasing number of tasks in the end-to-end value chain while they focus on what they do best: managing the overall chain. The next chapter explores why companies are turning to these external providers for support, and considers how this trend has created the need for an effective orchestrator of the end-to-end value chain—a role that CPOs are well positioned to assume.

CHAPTER 4

The Productivity Imperative: Orchestrating the End-to-End Value Chain

---

Main Messages

- Integrated companies will increasingly turn to external functional specialists that provide individual slivers of the integrated company's value chain at superior performance—the result of economies of skill and scale.
- The management of a company's end-to-end value chain will cross more and more company perimeters, requiring new management principles and attention to control value creation.
- Procurement is best positioned to assume the role of orchestrating the end-to-end chain since CPOs control the supplier relationship and are deeply embedded with their cross-functional value chain partners.

For decades, company strategists, academics, and management gurus have envisioned a future state in which globalization and specialization enable companies to focus on core competencies while sourcing noncore functions from best-in-class third parties. Today, this vision is not just becoming a *reality* by virtue of advances in technology and processes; it is becoming a *necessity* for maintaining a competitive edge in the global marketplace. To create value through cost reduction and innovation, companies must establish an integrated, end-to-end value chain that comprises best-in-class internal functions and external providers. A company's success will, in large measure, be determined by its ability to orchestrate this value chain that spans functions from market insight and product development to delivery and customer service. This orchestration entails designing and coordinating the overall value chain, as well as managing the individual value chain contributors (both external providers and internal functions) to ensure their effective interfacing and collaboration.

Many companies today have yet to master the ability to manage the full range of their external providers systematically and effectively. In many cases, different stakeholders within functional silos manage these providers, but they try to do so with no common management approach, service levels, or performance management framework.

What's more, few organizations take an end-to-end perspective on all internal and external providers to optimize the performance of the entire value chain. COOs, who are typically in a position to have an end-to-end perspective, often emphasize the optimization of internal functions over the comprehensive and tight management of external providers. In some cases, they may even be biased toward using internal resources rather than an external partner. Also, many of them have limited influence on upstream activities such as R&D and marketing.

What does this mean for procurement? The opportunities and pressures to source nondifferentiating parts of a company's value chain from external specialists are unlikely to abate. Thus, companies will generate increasing value by orchestrating their functional providers along a seamless end-to-end value chain. CPOs and the procurement function are ideally suited to lead this effort.

Because procurement interacts constantly with the external supply market, it is able to identify providers that can effectively fulfill the functional requirements of the company's value chain. Procurement has the processes and capabilities in place to manage vendors and integrate them seamlessly with the company's internal functions. And because procurement is already connected to all key company functions (for example, R&D, manufacturing, and service) along the value chain through cross-functional category teams, it is well positioned to play an integrating role among the functions and external providers. In fact, our Global Purchasing Excellence (GPE) survey showed that companies that already have strong cross-functional collaboration processes in place perform four times better on outsourcing and make-or-buy activities than those that don't.[1]

In addition to playing this integration role, the procurement function is also able to spot the value-creation opportunities in internal functions, benchmark them against the external market, and identify suitable providers through its ability to observe and assess the solutions offered by third parties.

---

[1]McKinsey analysis.

Last, procurement experts also have the relevant capabilities, such as negotiation and vendor management skills, required to manage the performance of external providers.

The Rise of Functional Specialists

Why is there potential to create value through the orchestrator's role? After all, sourcing parts of the value chain externally is nothing new for companies. Over the years, however, the scope of goods and services sourced externally and the complexity of the related decisions have risen to an entirely new level.

Outsourcing of significant, integrated parts of a company's value chain (in addition to parts and components that will require further processing) to external providers has transitioned from classic outsourcing—for instance, time-sharing or low-end processing services—to the sourcing of core business processes. For example, to address pressure from investors to improve their declining R&D productivity, several top-10 pharmaceutical companies have reconsidered their definition of core activities and publicly announced an aspiration to license up to 50 percent of their development portfolios from external sources, typically smaller biotech and pharmaceutical companies.[2]

For integrated companies to run their business competitively, the use of external outsourcing providers is now a prerequisite—not just an option. Companies in the low-margin consumer electronics and PC industries that do not leverage the massive scale that contract manufacturers have built over recent years are at a distinct disadvantage. Large-scale semiconductor foundries such as TSMC are among the few still able to put up the investment needed to build new fabrication plants. The capital expenditure required for a new fabrication plant has increased from U.S. $1.5 billion to U.S. $6.7 billion over the past 10 years, leaving very few players that can actually afford such ventures.[3]

Many companies have benefited by externally sourcing a wider range of activities, as illustrated by the growth in revenues per employee (RPE) in recent decades. In the automotive industry, for example, OEMs and suppliers approximately doubled their RPE from 1990 through 2000, as larger parts of the value chain were shifted to specialist contractors. From 2000 through 2010, average RPE of OEMs, as well as that of their

---

[2]Mark Egerton, "Outsourcing R&D—Ride the Outsourcing Wave," *Pharmaceutical Formulation & Quality*, April/May 2012.
[3]McKinsey analysis.

suppliers, grew by more than 60 percent.[4] Some of these gains can be attributed to model mix changes and retail price increases. However, the tripling of RPE in a 20-year period could not have been possible without large productivity increases, which were, to a significant extent, driven by outsourcing. OEMs started by modularizing their components and, using a step-by-step approach, they shifted their in-house engineering and manufacturing to tier 1 suppliers.

And start-ups in other industries have managed to achieve RPEs that executives in the automotive industry can only dream about. For example, Craigslist generates U.S. $115 million in revenues with not many more than 30 employees. The company leverages external partners for most of its value chain functions.[5]

Companies such as Skype, Coca-Cola, Procter & Gamble (P&G), and Apple are among the leaders in recognizing that their success doesn't depend on doing everything themselves. These companies have defined the specific functions they're truly good at—typically, product development or marketing. And they focus internal resources on these functions while they tightly orchestrate an end-to-end value chain that includes many well-managed external partners and suppliers. "We are in the business of building and creating brands," said A. G. Lafley, former CEO of P&G, in an interview, not mentioning manufacturing, distribution, or even product development.[6]

Integrated companies such as these develop, market, and deliver their products to end customers along an end-to-end value chain. The functions along this value chain include market insight generation, product development, product management, sourcing and manufacturing, distribution and logistics, and marketing and sales. Leading integrated companies source well-defined elements of their value chain—for example, distribution and logistics, manufacturing, and development—from functional specialists. These integrated companies don't pursue functional excellence throughout their own organizations. Instead, they source excellent functions readily available in the market while concentrating their efforts on tight management of the external partners as part of a seamless, end-to-end value chain—from product development to service.

The growth rates of specialists that provide services for core functions are also impressive. R&D-focused original design manufacturers (ODMs) in consumer electronics, for example, grew at an average annual rate of

---

[4]McKinsey analysis.

[5]Noah Davies, "Craigslist Revenue Pegged at $115 Million This Year, Dropping for the First Time in 9 Years," *Business Insider*, October 7, 2011.

[6]Robert Berner, "P&G: New and Improved," *Bloomberg Businessweek*, July 6, 2003.

17 percent from 2002 through 2010, contract manufacturers grew at 26 percent, and specialists in marketing and sales enjoyed growth rates ranging from 10 to 17 percent. Indeed, we have found that growth rates of functional specialists have exceeded those of integrated companies by factors ranging from 2 to 4, depending on the industry (see Exhibit 4.1). In the consumer electronics industry, for example, functional specialists grew at a compound annual growth rate (CAGR) of 22 percent from 2002 through 2010, while integrated companies grew at a CAGR of only 8 percent (a factor of 2.7). In the automotive and pharmaceutical industries, the growth rates of functional specialists exceeded those of integrated companies that source from these specialists by even larger factors (4.2 and 3.2, respectively).[7]

Revenue growth CAGR, 2002–2010, percent

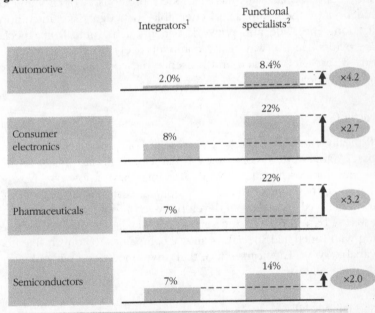

EXHIBIT 4.1 Revenue Growth of Integrators versus Functional Specialists by Industry. Growth of functional specialists like contract manufacturers or research companies suggests a strong trend to outsource noncore activities.

[1]An integrator is defined as the primary governor of the value chain, typically owning the brand.
[2]A functional specialist is defined as a company providing a service fulfilling a partial need in the value chain (e.g., contract manufacturers, logistics providers, contract research organizations).
Source: McKinsey Corporate Performance Analysis Tool, team analysis.

---

[7]McKinsey analysis.

These growth rates reflect the significant synergies that can be achieved by executing and optimizing only certain functions or parts of an integrator's value chain. These benefits can be understood in terms of operational scale, factor cost, and specialized skill.

Operational Scale

Functional specialists achieve economies of scale by bundling demand for their services from various companies. An integrated company cannot capture these economies of scale for the expert's specific service because the service represents only one step in the company's long value chain. Semiconductor foundries and contract manufacturers are the best examples of functional specialists that create synergies from sheer operational scale, as discussed previously. By pooling demand, functional experts are also better able to hedge risks and improve utilization. The scale and network benefits achievable from specialization are evident in the way many companies rely on global logistics providers, whose global reach and presence the companies leverage to access world markets.

Factor Cost

Typically, functional specialists can offer companies access to a lower cost base. Many Western companies in particular still have many of their facilities in high-cost locations. While they may have a low cost base for some activities, they almost never have optimal costs for all of them. It's easier for functional specialists to develop low-cost footprints to achieve the lowest cost base for a specific service and quality level. Furthermore, working with functional specialists allows companies to convert fixed costs into variable costs: They can reduce their investments and pay only for services they actually use.

Specialized Skill

Specialist companies can also develop distinctive functional capabilities by focusing on only a few core activities. Examples include contract research organizations (CROs), which grew as an industry because biotech companies had limited internal-development capabilities, and research agencies, which amass specific knowledge and data relevant for marketing and product management departments of integrated companies. Specialist companies are better positioned to continually invest in technology and upgrade their capabilities, enabling them to deliver innovation faster and in a more cost-effective manner.

What's Driving the Shift?

Two key trends are driving the growth of sourcing from external functional specialists: competitive market pressures that increase the need to streamline a company's value chain and the greater availability of offerings to meet this need.

Market Pressures

Business acceleration and glocalization (which we discussed in Chapter 3) are the primary market pressures driving the shift to functional specialists.

BUSINESS ACCELERATION Companies can no longer do everything themselves if they hope to keep up with the accelerated pace of business. There are too many pieces to put in place—fast. Companies must continually look for the best solutions available in the supply market, and this means sourcing functional expertise from external providers.

The accelerated pace of business is reflected in the dramatic reduction in duration of product life cycles. In the automotive industry, for example, product life cycles have shortened by almost 20 percent over the past two decades.[8] Brands such as BMW have been even more aggressive. At the same time, the annual number of new models introduced has increased significantly, from an annual average of 0.7 per automaker in the 1990s to more than two per automaker today.[9]

How are automotive companies leveraging external providers to speed up their product introductions? Consider, for example, Magna Steyr, which has helped automotive OEMs launch products faster than they could have done it themselves, given resource limitations within their product-development function and capacity constraints in production. In 2003, while under pressure to launch a compact SUV quickly, BMW contracted with Magna Steyr to help develop and build its X3 model from concept to production. Magna Steyr achieved this goal by flexibly assigning 500 engineers to replicate BMW's engineering, production, and quality processes. It had similarly taken over the complete engineering-to-production process of several other major OEMs. This example also shows another benefit: the ability to increase flexibility in the resources deployed. Automakers can choose whether they should create each new model in-house or to leverage specialists—and decide which specialists to work with.[10]

---

[8]McKinsey analysis.
[9]McKinsey analysis.
[10]Gail Edmondson, "Look Who's Building Bimmers," *Bloomberg Businessweek*, November 30, 2003.

GLOCALIZATION As discussed earlier, to tap the potential of emerging markets, global companies need to go local by tailoring their products and go-to-market models much more to the needs of local markets. This requires the flexibility and speed to react to changes in local consumer requirements. This, in turn, means that companies must build differentiated end-to-end value chains to serve the needs of their local customers around the globe.

To accomplish this, integrated companies are sourcing from local functional specialists in their respective target markets. Specialists that have a deep understanding of the local environment can provide their element of the integrated company's value chain more effectively and cost efficiently than most integrated companies. In most cases, this includes local sales-and-service channel partners, marketing agencies, and design houses that can help global companies create products and services tailored to local markets.

Greater Availability of Offerings

Business acceleration and glocalization create increasing demand for functional specialists, and integrated companies are finding that this need can be met by a much greater number of offerings. This greater availability is driven by the commoditization of functional excellence and the standardization of process and IT solutions.

COMMODITIZATION OF FUNCTIONAL EXCELLENCE For many critical elements of the value chain, specialized skills are now ubiquitous in the external market, and commoditization of functional excellence is a result. Consider such simple support services as facility management, internal mail operations, cleaning, and canteen services: Most large corporations today rely on external providers to deliver these services. This is increasingly true of other core functions such as manufacturing and development. In fact, companies that provide these services are among the world's largest and fastest growing. Consequently, integrated companies today have many sourcing choices that can provide the scale, cost, and skill benefits described earlier.

This is prominently illustrated by the emergence of electronic manufacturing service (EMS) providers and ODMs. These functional specialists design and produce a wide range of devices—including mobile phones and notebooks—in higher volumes than would have been possible for any single OEM. Today, Foxconn, Synnex, and Quanta are among the largest corporations in the world—and none of them is a household brand name. In fact, Foxconn, which builds products for companies that include virtually all major consumer electronics and PC brands, is the world's second-largest private employer after Wal-Mart. An estimated 40 percent of all consumer-electronics products produced globally come from Foxconn's factories.[11] Foxconn's sheer size-and-scale advantage is a differentiator that now presents a clear barrier to integrated companies that consider running their business without leveraging Foxconn's support as a supplier.

Wistron, another example, offers product design, prototyping, and testing services to integrated consumer-electronics companies. The company has grown by double digits annually since it was spun off from Acer in 2002, and now reports annual revenues of U.S. $21 billion.[12]

These specialist providers are at the leading edge, applying well-known best practices in product development (concurrent engineering, agile), manufacturing (lean), and distribution (network design, hub-and-spoke) at scale. Few integrated companies can provide these capabilities in-house at the same level as functional specialists, especially because specialists increasingly offer benefits of scale and low costs that are hard to ignore.

There are, however, also two potential drawbacks to extensive use of the more advanced specialists. The integrated company risks losing the internal capabilities to challenge functional specialists, and the external providers may move beyond their specialization to become competitors. One role of the orchestrator is to contain such risks.

STANDARDIZATION OF IT AND BUSINESS PROCESSES By reducing transaction and interaction costs, the standardization of business processes, data structures, and interfaces has enabled companies to more quickly and more effectively source parts of their value chains from external parties. For example, following a major IT-standardization initiative, Unilever began to outsource many of its administrative functions—including accounts payable, travel expense management, and bill-to-cash processing—to IBM.[13]

At the same time, new collaboration techniques have emerged that allow companies to connect to suppliers and customers along the value chain more easily for activities such as concurrent engineering, collaborative forecasting, communication, and exchange. This promotes increasingly rapid innovation and shorter product life cycles. For example, InnoCentive, which was founded in 2001, provides an interface between companies that need problems solved and external problem solvers. Currently, there are more than 230,000 problem solvers registered

---

[11]"How the U.S. Lost Out on iPhone Work," *New York Times*, January 21, 2012.

[12]"2001 Annual Reports," Wistron, accessed February 6, 2013, www.wistron.com/investors/annual_reports.htm.

[13]"IBM Global Process Services Unilever," IBM, accessed February 6, 2013, www.apdsi.pt/uploads/news/id487/IBM%20APDSI%20Novembro%202011%20Final.pdf.

at InnoCentive, a sizable workforce comprising experts on nearly every topic. A number of major corporate clients have used InnoCentive to over-come obstacles in product development faster and more cheaply by sourc-ing solutions from its network of problem solvers.[14]

The Need for an Orchestrator

As companies increasingly turn to functional specialists to source critical parts of their value chains, the end-to-end integration of both internal and external parties becomes essential for success. It will not be enough to merely optimize the relationship between external partners and the cor-responding internal functions. Market leadership will require orchestrat-ing the web of interconnected relationships throughout the value chain to achieve seamless, effective performance. Companies will need an orches-trator to ensure that individual outsourcing relationships deliver on their promised value, mitigate the associated risks, and capture the full value from the interconnected network of internal and external providers.

As more functions are sourced from external specialist providers, ensur-ing that all these individual arrangements deliver on the promised value has become critical to a company's performance. Companies are finding that their goals for cost reduction and quality improvement are not easily achieved. Overall, the need to achieve greater effectiveness in outsourcing will be among the major issues confronting businesses during the next five years.[15] Our research suggests that more professional management of out-sourcing yields higher earnings before interest and taxes (EBIT) margins. In the chemical and health care sectors, for example, EBIT margins of compa-nies that score low on outsourcing are approximately four percentage points lower than margins of medium- or high-scoring companies, while for finan-cial institutions the difference is five percentage points.[16]

Outsourcing risk mitigation is also increasingly important. In an unpre-dictable and volatile economy, outsourcing contracts must be set to adjust to the changing environment. For example, currency fluctuations alone could drastically affect the impact of a typical multiyear outsourcing contract.

---

[14]Thomas W. Malone, Robert J. Laubacher, and Tammy Johns, "The Big Idea: The Age of Hyperspecialization," *Harvard Business Review*, July 2011, 2.

[15]Kathleen Goolsby, "The Big Challenge That Will Reshape Outsourcing from 2011–2015," *Outsourcing Center*, accessed January 2, 2011, www.outsourcing -center.com/2011-01-the-big-challenge-that-will-reshape-outsourcing-from-2011 -2015-article-42428.html.

[16]McKinsey analysis.

Furthermore, effective management of functional providers along one seamless chain with optimized handover points and cross-provider synergies will become a key activity for value creation. In many companies, different stakeholders manage individual providers (for example, the IT function manages IT service providers, and the supply chain operations function manages the global-logistics providers). Standard procedures and best practices are not codified and applied throughout the organization. Few companies have a comprehensive view of all their large-scale external service providers and partners, and few can manage the multitude of relationships in a way that optimizes the end-to-end impact.

Why does this matter? A poorly performing function along the end-to-end value chain can drag down overall performance. Handover problems between functions—internally or externally provided—can negatively affect overall performance. Functions may not pass the baton in an effective and timely manner, leading to miscommunication and delays, customer dissatisfaction, rework, and funding imbalances. Coordination among functions is also critical to ensure alignment on the provision of goods and services and the timing of new-product launches and marketing campaigns. Consider the example of a consumer goods company that was aggressively growing one of its new categories. Product development optimized product cost, sales optimized shelf space and sell-in to stores, and supply chain optimized inventories. But nobody looked at the entire value chain. When executives eventually adopted an integrated, end-to-end perspective, they found that costs from obsolete parts and semifinished and finished goods along the full chain had turned what should have been reasonable gross profits into massive net losses. The remedy was clear: The company had to think about and optimize all functions from an integrated, end-to-end perspective.

A Natural Role for Procurement

To address the challenges of value delivery and risk mitigation, orchestrators must perform a number of important tasks. They must apply external market insights to identify services for which external functional specialists may be superior to internal functions. They must identify and qualify the right external providers, and seamlessly integrate their services into their company's value chain. Orchestrators must also maintain a holistic perspective on all external provider relationships, ensuring they are managed using a common framework. And, as orchestrators are integrating both internal and external parties along the end-to-end chain, they also need to ensure that interfaces are working and any conflicts that arise are being resolved.

As this set of activities suggests, the orchestrator role has a broad mandate. It includes defining the objectives and scope of vendor involvement, collecting and defining the business requirements, selecting the vendors and negotiating the contracts on the basis of detailed service-level agreements, and ensuring that mechanisms and capabilities are in place to manage internal demand. Rigid performance management is required to review the value delivered from sourcing decisions on a regular basis.

Procurement in its role as supply entrepreneur is the natural owner of the orchestrator role. No other function is as close to the external-supply market or as well positioned to identify providers that can fulfill the functional requirements of the company's value chain more effectively. Procurement already manages vendors and integrates them with the company's internal functions. And because procurement is typically well connected to all key company functions along the value chain (with, for example, R&D, manufacturing, and service) through cross-functional category teams, it is well positioned to play an integrating role among the functions and external providers. At the same time, it is able to spot value-creation opportunities at internal functions, benchmark them against the external market, and identify suitable providers through its ability to observe solutions offered by third parties. Procurement experts also have the relevant capabilities, such as negotiation and vendor management skills, required to manage external providers for performance.

What Are the Possibilities?

Several companies have recognized the need to improve the end-to-end value-chain orchestration, and they have found the natural owner for the orchestrator's role in their procurement function. The examples of Qoros Auto and Apple help illuminate the possibilities with respect to expanded orchestration activities, as well as the CPO's opportunity to contribute to, if not lead, these initiatives.

Qoros

This Chinese passenger car start-up has designed its business model on the basis of relationships with best-practice value-chain partners such as Magna Steyr or Semcon. Other companies should find the possibilities intriguing to watch and consider.

Founded in 2007 as a joint venture between a local carmaker and a foreign private-equity company, Qoros set for itself the challenge of making good use of best practices from the fast-moving consumer-goods industry in its automotive business model. It brought together a world-class management team whose members average more than 20 years of experience with leading Western carmakers. The company's first move was to define a clear set of differentiating factors for the new brand. These included styling and safety, which led the company to hire leading European experts from German and Swedish carmakers for its in-house staff. In all nondifferentiating areas, the company strove to match international standards, but it did not seek to create a unique selling point for its customers. In these areas, the focus would be on maximizing the company's efficiency and flexibility by leveraging the know-how of external partners.

For this approach to succeed, the in-house engineers had to lead the launch of the first product while simultaneously initiating the development of the models to be launched in the following months and years. Most automakers would dedicate separate core teams to each program, which requires duplicating, and often underutilizing, core resources and expertise. The CPO, Mark Zhou (a former senior executive at Lear, an automotive-components supplier), was given the mandate to select and develop the entire supply base for the first family of Qoros products. Zhou worked closely with his company's lead engineers to create a model that would allow the company to leverage fewer than 200 in-house engineers to develop a full range of products, while relying heavily on external engineering partners.

This heavy reliance on external partners made effective orchestration a prerequisite for success. One critical success factor was the Qoros team's sharing of key performance indicators (KPIs) and related goals with the external partners. In the development contract, Zhou required the engineering partner to create a program organization that mirrored the company's. Engineers from Qoros and the external partner were assigned to each module. The performance of each engineer assigned to a module was measured using the same deadlines for completing the development of the components, according to the specifications agreed on, and the same targets for cost and weight. The next step consisted of transforming the weekly program management decision meetings, traditionally internal sessions, into joint working sessions with the engineering partner. In such meetings, the module engineers from Qoros and the partner would jointly present status updates, highlight risks and roadblocks, and get guidance from the joint leadership of Qoros and the engineering partner. A senior engineering leader attended each weekly meeting.

Despite the robust process and organization setup, many issues that arose during the development of such a complex effort naturally required adjustments to the partnership's contract terms. To prevent the program meetings from becoming negotiation sessions, Zhou's team and their engineering partners held separate change management sessions with their senior counterparts to determine how best to manage changes. These meetings led to the implementation of a stringent target-setting and incentive scheme for the external partners. Another key aspect was the introduction of supplier development resources that would liaise with the engineering providers in monitoring the development of each module.

After the earliest development phase, Zhou initiated discussions with other engineering providers to minimize the risks of overdependency on the initial partner. When the development of the second Qoros vehicle began, the collaboration model was stepped up further, with different modules being assigned to different external engineering partners. The increased complexity proved a challenge for the Qoros engineering team, who had to ensure consistency among different interfaces that were, in principle, competing with one another. As a result, the partnership contracts had to be adapted to set more prescriptive targets. Full success could be achieved only through the rigorous defining and tracking of targets by Zhou's team, along with extensive coaching and guidance of the resources by the Qoros engineering leadership.

The company's effort to leverage external specialists didn't stop with engineering. Qoros has also started looking for external partners to develop its sales and after-sales network. Building on the outstanding partnership Zhou built between the external partners and the company's internal resources, this ambitious team is currently on track to launch its first product in 2013, followed by one or two new versions per year thereafter. Although the long-term outcome is still to be proven, the successful orchestration of the engineering partnerships has paved the way for Zhou and his colleagues in the top management team to transform how automotive companies operate.[17]

The Qoros approach mirrors the way many Internet start-up companies designed their business models. Many of these companies had the chance to start their business without the legacy of an in-house staff in functional areas. They explicitly decided to tap into the growing pool of externally available expertise for most of their functional needs along the value chain, focusing on what they considered their core activities: customer acquisition and the tight management of the outsourced parts of the business.

Apple

Tim Cook is one of the best-known examples of a leader stepping up to the role of end-to-end orchestrator. Cook joined Apple in the mid-1990s as a senior vice president of operations and became its COO in 2005. In these roles, he was instrumental in optimizing Apple's entire supply

---

[17]Interview with Mark Zhou, Qoros, January 2013.

chain. He closed "factories and warehouses around the world and instead established relationships with contract manufacturers."[18] Apple outsourced its production to contract manufacturers such as Foxconn, which not only offered significant savings potential but also helped free up resources and convert fixed costs to variable costs. Ultimately, this helped improve Apple's "inventory and margins, which are the envy of the industry."[19]

Apple maintains control over nearly every step along the value chain. The company demands detailed cost breakdowns for all product components it buys; sends engineers into supplier companies to help change processes so the product launch is just right; in some cases, buys the full market supply of key components to secure supply and block competitors' access; and tightly manages critical tier 2 and tier 3 suppliers of key components, including displays, LEDs, and chip sets. It also manages vendors' material choices and EMS providers' production schedules. The orchestration is so tight and extensive that Apple places electronic monitors into some parts boxes at supplier sites to allow remote monitoring of production speed and discourage product theft.[20] Additionally, Apple uses its own retail stores to achieve full and instant visibility of consumer demand, allowing for the real-time adjustment of manufacturers' production and shipping cycles.[21]

Stepping Up to the Role

These examples demonstrate the tremendous potential in capturing value from tighter orchestration of external providers and internal functions. What does it take for CPOs to assume the orchestrator's role? The orchestrator must take responsibility for coordinating the interactions among internal parties and external functional specialists and must manage the latter for high performance. The successful orchestrator builds on procurement's existing cross-functional mechanisms, such as cross-functional category teams and strategic category councils in which cross-functional company leaders decide on category strategies.

---

[18]Adam Lashinsky, "The Genius Behind Steve," *CNN Money*, accessed March 22, 2013, http://money.cnn.com/2008/11/09/technology/cook_apple.fortune/index.htm.
[19]Erica Ogg, "What Will Apple under CEO Tim Cook Look Like?" *Bloomberg Businessweek*, August 24, 2011.
[20]Adam Satariano and Peter Burrows, "Apple's Supply Chain Secret: Hoard Lasers," *Bloomberg Businessweek*, November 3, 2011.
[21]Robert J. Bowman, "Of Zippers, Matzos and Closed Supply Chains," *SupplyChain Brain*, accessed July 16, 2012, www.supplychainbrain.com/content/blogs/think-tank/blog/article/font-size2of-zippers-matzos-and-closed-supply-chainsfont/.

Building upon the existing cross-functional mechanisms, additional changes are required for CPOs to assume an orchestrating role among internal and external value chain partners. CPOs need to make three thrusts iteratively: securing an initial mandate from the CEO, expanding the mandate by proving to internal stakeholders that the CPO's orchestrating role adds value, and taking an entrepreneurial stance to build the required new capabilities to sustain the results.

Secure the Mandate from the CEO

A mandate from the CEO is essential for CPOs who aim to step up to a broader provider-management and orchestration role. As discussed in Chapter 1, "The Drivers of Sustainable Procurement Performance," in most industries the CPO should have a seat at the table when the relevant business strategies are defined. Our GPE data suggest that excellence in outsourcing requires the CPO's involvement in the relevant strategy-definition activities. Procurement organizations that score high on their alignment with company strategy are three times more likely to demonstrate above-average performance in outsourcing and in make-or-buy processes as well.[22]

Procurement organizations typically earn an expanded mandate through proven successes in classical category and vendor management. Our GPE survey found that procurement functions that excel at these more traditional tasks are almost four times as likely to play a significant role in outsourcing management.

CPOs must ensure that they can make the case for an expansion of their mandate toward more integrated management of value chain partners. For example, the mandate could explicitly include the following: regularly benchmarking internal functions against external providers, managing the day-to-day interactions with large-scale EMS and IT outsourcing providers, and assuming accountability for the seamless, end-to-end performance management of all stakeholders along the internal and external value chain. Typically, the CPO receives this broadened mandate directly from the CEO.

Willie Deese, formerly the CPO at Merck, was given this broader mandate, along with a promotion to president of the company's manufacturing division in 2005. That year, Merck announced its plan to shut 5 of its 31 manufacturing facilities worldwide and reduce operations at a number of other sites as part of a major restructuring that included an increase in outsourcing to fine-chemical makers. "The strategy involves substantial change in the way we commercialize, manufacture, and supply our products," Deese said. "The main components of the strategy are creating a seamless global facility network that combines the best of Merck manufacturing with

---

[22]McKinsey analysis.

the increasingly sophisticated manufacturing capabilities of key external suppliers." Key elements established under the orchestrating role included implementing an integrated lean production system, reconfiguring the manufacturing operations to form a network that was better aligned to flexible demand shifts, broadening the foreign supplier base to leverage price efficiencies, and focusing internal manufacturing resources on pivotal activities that would give the company a competitive advantage.[23]

The CPO's broadened mandate can, at times, overlap the mandates of other functional leaders. Imagine a company that has distributed most of its value chain to functional specialists such as design houses, contract manufacturers, logistics providers, and distributors. The CPO manages these vendors with his or her procurement team and ensures that they work together seamlessly along the value chain. As more operational functions are outsourced and managed by the CPO, he or she assumes additional responsibilities that may have been associated with a COO. Over time, the CPO's role will look more like that of a COO, the key difference being that external parties provide most of the managed operations. Looking at this evolution of roles another way, COOs will find that skills currently applied by CPOs will become significantly more important to their own roles in the future.

In addressing these challenges, CPOs should give priority to forging strong ties and relationships with the leaders of all internal functions. Because external partners are managed in concert with the internal function that employs the provider, CPOs must be close to the stakeholders in, for example, R&D and manufacturing. It is also important to maintain a good relationship with the head of corporate strategy, who may be a powerful ally in defining core and noncore parts of the business.

Tim Cook's success at Apple illustrates the power of having a clear mandate from the CEO to achieve end-to-end integration across internal functions and external partners. Cook, who had led procurement at Compaq, was hired by Steve Jobs specifically to clean up Apple's severely troubled manufacturing, distribution, and supply functions. As Jobs recalled: "Tim Cook came out of procurement, which is just the right background for what we needed."[24] This mandate gave Cook the authority to completely revamp Apple's value chain, phase out its manufacturing footprint, and develop close relationships with external manufacturing partners. Ultimately, Cook's success led to his appointment as CEO. Although Cook was not Apple's CPO, his initiatives exemplify the types of activities that CPOs should pursue as orchestrators.

---

[23]Robert Westervelt, "Merck Restructuring Will Lead to More Outsourcing," *Chemical Week*, November 30, 2005.

[24]Walter Isaacson, *Steve Jobs* (New York: Simon & Schuster, 2011), 360.

Demonstrate the Value Added to Key Stakeholders

In an iterative process, the initial mandate from the top needs to be followed by fast and visible wins that add value to business stakeholders. This, in turn, can help to enhance the mandate. Proving value often begins by establishing a track record of better management of classical outsourcing relationships (for instance, call center services and IT) by, for example, implementing more comprehensive performance management of vendors. This might include a centrally coordinated alignment of all vendors' objectives and KPIs against the primary company's KPIs.

Once the procurement organization demonstrates its ability to orchestrate the value chain, CPOs should strive to assume responsibilities both earlier in the outsourcing process (for example, scoping the specific parts of the business to outsource) and later (for example, managing transitions to new providers). CPOs should also start bringing forward new outsourcing ideas, backed by solid facts on potential providers, external benchmarks for the internal functions being considered for outsourcing, and business cases that set out the benefits and risks. This can extend to helping the corporate strategy function and the board define the company's core competencies and identifying the competencies that should be outsourced to functional specialists over time. The broad scope of these activities highlights the need for a strong mandate for the CPO. In a virtuous cycle, this mandate will expand with the successful execution of these activities and will, in turn, enable the CPO to further expand the scope of his or her orchestration efforts.

Operationally, CPOs can add value by scouting for and assessing new vendors and structuring and negotiating deals, as well as by managing providers on behalf of the company. In fact, proper supplier performance management proves to be one of the key factors in excellent outsourcing. Our GPE data suggest that companies that perform at a high or very high level on supplier performance management are almost three times as likely to be good at management of outsourcing.[25]

Build New Capabilities

Today, very few procurement organizations have the capabilities to challenge internal customers with external benchmarks, manage large-scale external service providers, or engage in discussions to distinguish the company's core and noncore activities with the head of strategy and the board. To take on these tasks from outside their comfort zone and step

---

[25]McKinsey analysis.

up to the orchestrator role, CPOs and their teams must strengthen their positions and capabilities in the following areas.

DEVELOPING AN IN-DEPTH UNDERSTANDING OF CORE AND SUPPORT PROCESSES AND THE RELATED PROVIDER INDUSTRIES The orchestrator must take an objective and neutral view of internal functions (both core and non-core) and have a good perspective on the relevant supply markets. These insights will help the orchestrator select the areas in which it makes most sense to push for more sourcing from external specialists—support processes, nondifferentiating core processes, and areas in which external vendors have used scale and skill benefits to leap ahead of internal functions in terms of productivity and quality. This entails both staying close to functional leaders to understand their cost and value drivers and their constraints and being aware of providers' offerings, economics, and relative advantages.

ANALYZING AND BENCHMARKING INTERNAL FUNCTIONS AND EXTERNAL PROVIDERS On a regular basis, internal functions should be put into direct competition with external specialist providers in order to introduce competitive pressures. This generally involves defining the right KPIs and performance management mechanisms for both internal and external functions. Comparing performance of internal functions against external providers requires an indisputable fact base and analytical rigor. In many cases, internal functions do not have a favorable opinion of outsourcing opportunities. Having a discussion that is built on clear facts and business cases is the only way to obtain neutral, unbiased opinions and to maintain trust in the relationship.

IDENTIFYING AND QUALIFYING THE RIGHT EXTERNAL PROVIDERS AND SEAMLESSLY INTEGRATING THEIR SERVICES INTO THE COMPANY'S VALUE CHAIN Identifying and qualifying the right external providers are classical procurement capabilities, while seamlessly integrating their services into the company's value chain extends responsibility into facilitating how the external providers are most effectively connected to internal processes and functions. This includes the definition of clear interfaces, deliverables, and collaboration mechanisms. Initiatives to drive continual improvement of the interface are equally part of it, as well as initiatives to optimize the work and task allocation among internal and external stakeholders.

MAINTAINING A HOLISTIC PERSPECTIVE ON ALL EXTERNAL PROVIDER RELATIONSHIPS, ENSURING THAT THEY ARE MANAGED USING A COMMON FRAMEWORK As the orchestrator, procurement must work with various external vendors simultaneously and maintain a clear view of deliveries, performance and quality levels, and specific provider issues that may affect the company, such as new regulations, tier 2 supply shortages, and competitive threats. To do this effectively for a large number of providers, orchestrators must be able to develop and establish common management frameworks that guide the management and escalation of issues according to consistent and predefined rules.

APPLYING SKILLS FOR NETWORKING AND RELATIONSHIP AND STAKEHOLDER MANAGEMENT TO ALIGN PARTIES ON OBJECTIVES AND PLANS CPOs should follow the example of successful category managers who use their influence over cross-functional stakeholders to create impact in areas such as new-supplier introduction, product standardization, and demand and specification challenging. This capability is becoming more important, because many end-to-end orchestration issues require aligning different internal and external parties along the value chain on issues such as priorities, activities, concrete targets, and interfaces. Consequently, orchestrators have a role in identifying and resolving conflicts between value chain participants. Imagine faulty deliveries that cause disruptions at downstream providers, or providers that fail to exchange relevant data with other parties in the chain. The orchestrator serves as a clearinghouse for addressing issues such as these.

DEVELOPING SKILLS TO MANAGE LARGE-SCALE, HIGH-VALUE PROJECTS Managing complex vendor relationships and contracts requires another level of project management skills typically expected of a category manager. For example, it involves an in-depth understanding of the activities outsourced; the key control points and value levers; all interdependencies with other internal functions and external providers and subproviders; and contractual details, including performance and change-request management.

Companies That Are Riding the Wave

In less than 10 years, **Skype** has become the world's largest phone operator, serving 660 million Internet protocol (IP) phone subscribers globally. With merely 500 people on its payroll, Skype could not have achieved such a high growth rate if it had chosen to develop all the required knowledge and capabilities in-house.

Skype started with software development by Bluemoon Interactive programmers in Estonia, and today the company uses functional excellence and ready-made solutions from various third parties.

Skype also lets other organizations and individuals support the development of its own product. According to Sten Tamkivi, the company's head of operations and general manager, "We may have only 200 engineers, but there are another 3,000 people out there working on solutions for Skype. It is thanks to this community of developers that over 400 Skype-compatible applications have arisen—from simple voice mail to a CRM [customer relationship management] solution for companies." Skype achieves a similar leverage effect through widespread cooperation among its network of hardware manufacturers, including some of the global market leaders. Tamkivi said, "Developers wishing to integrate Skype into their hardware send us a sample. If the product meets our standards, then it may bear the Skype brand." This approach leaves Skype employees to focus on what really creates differentiating value: managing and orchestrating the end-to-end value chain. In May 2011, Microsoft announced a U.S. $8.5 billion bid for the company—US $17 million per employee.

India's **Airtel** (Bharti Airtel Limited) is one of the world's three largest single-country telecommunications operators. Today, it has more than 250 million customers, revenues of approximately U.S. $13 billion, and a healthy EBIT margin of more than 15 percent. It has built its business on the basis of the firm belief that its low revenue-per-user environment required building only as much capacity as it needed to satisfy customer demand. This meant that Airtel would not build excess capacity and wait for customers to come. Instead, it had to negotiate outcome-based contracts with multiple external specialists so that it would have the flexibility to buy only as much capacity as demand required.

Pursuing this strategy, Airtel outsourced its network to ZTE, NSN, Huawei, Alcatel-Lucent, and Ericsson; its customer service to Nortel; and its IT services to IBM. Specialists, including Mphasis, Firstsource, and Teleperformance, run the company's call centers. Yahoo! and Google, among others, provide analytics of customer behavior.

Airtel tightly manages all of these providers along an end-to-end integrated KPI system that includes top-level customer KPIs (such as customer satisfaction or call drop rates), as well as operational KPIs by area. It also adapts KPI values to local market requirements. This synchronized system and all service-level agreements are maintained by the global supply-chain organization. Outsourcing partners are strategically involved from concept and design through the launch of the operations of the respective functional services they provide.

Cross-functional committees comprising functional representatives and members of the global supply-chain organization oversee the providers' performance.

Strategic outsourcing and end-to-end integration have enabled Airtel to realize impressive growth in India's low-revenue environment. S. Asokan, head of the global supply-chain organization, said, "These providers are much better equipped to run our operations than we are: They are more capable, efficient, and specialized. At the same time, we can concentrate exclusively on our customers!"[26]

In many cases, bringing these capabilities into the organization requires hiring more highly skilled people who have worked for internal customers or providers. In some cases, category managers can step up to assume these capabilities.

■ ■ ■

The need to drive innovation and productivity has forced companies to rethink what they are best at, focus their internal work on these areas, and hand over other parts of the value chain to specialists. For CPOs, this creates significant opportunities to lead increasingly complex sourcing relationships and manage these external relations to maximize value. A CPO must define himself or herself as follows:

- The seamless, end-to-end integrator of internal functions and the external parties that will take on an increasing share of the value chain.
- A well-networked scout seeking to identify how external parties can create value for the enterprise in terms of both cost reduction and innovation along the full value chain.
- The orchestrator of all relationships along the chain—maximizing control, collaboration, and value extraction through new technologies.
- A challenger of internal company functions with respect to their ability to add value and enhance competitiveness relative to external providers.

---

[26]Interview with S. Asokan, Airtel, October 2012.

- A thought leader and strategic architect in determining the company's core functions, building on an in-depth understanding of the potential competitiveness and the value contribution of external providers.

To achieve these aspirations, CPOs must be in the flow of information and data and develop insights that will promote better collaboration along the value chain. Success requires tapping into and shaping the emerging world of big data and advanced analytics. The next chapter discusses how these emerging opportunities not only support this collaboration but also add value in myriad other ways.

Big Data and the Global Grid: Procurement's New Role in Data-Driven Decision Making

<table>
<tr><td>

Main Messages

- Available data and communication bandwidth will continue to increase by orders of magnitude in the next few years.
- Big data and the global grid will have a profound impact on businesses by enabling new insights, collaboration at scale, and superior, data-driven decision making.
- Already, procurement uses internal and external data for decision making and communication bandwidth for supplier integration and management. The advent of even more data and bandwidth will strengthen and expand procurement's role.

</td></tr>
</table>

The amount of digitally available data in the world has been exploding upward. Analyzing large data sets—so-called big data—will become a prerequisite for competitiveness, underpinning new waves of productivity growth, innovation, and consumer surplus. Amazon's recommendation engine supports shoppers in finding the right products to buy. Sentiment analysis of social media and tweets helps predict movie successes and spot company image issues early. And analysis of mass patient data alongside treatment effectiveness analysis yields insights for health care providers to save thousands of lives and millions of dollars. The increasing volume and detail of information captured by enterprises, the rise of multimedia and social media, and even the upswing in connectivity among inanimate objects will fuel more exponential growth in data for the foreseeable future. Grappling with the implications of big data will not be the domain of just a few data-oriented managers. Rather, every leader in every sector will need to reorient his or her work to harness the power of big data.

Amid this explosion of data, the global economy is growing ever more connected into one global grid. Complex flows of capital, goods, information, and people are creating an interlinked network that spans geographies, social groups, and economies in ways that permit large-scale interactions at any moment. Money, goods, data, and people now cross borders in huge volumes and at unprecedented speed. Since 1990, trade flows have grown 1.5 times faster than global gross domestic product (GDP). Cross-border capital flows have expanded at three times the rate of GDP growth.[1] The volume of global information exchanged has increased significantly in the past decade and is expected to grow fourfold from 2011 through 2016—to 1,100 exabytes (see Exhibit 5.1). (One exabyte

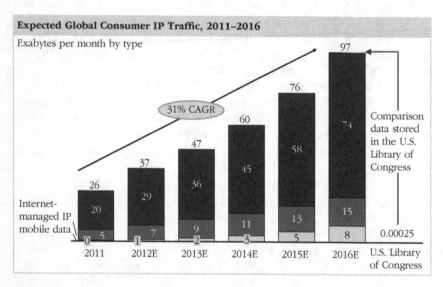

EXHIBIT 5.1 Torrent of Global Internet Information Exchange Growing at 31 Percent CAGR

Source: 2012 Cisco Virtual Indexing Forecast and Methodology; U.S. Library of Congress.

---

[1]Peter Bisson, Elizabeth Stephenson, and S. Patrick Viguerie, "The Global Grid," *McKinseyQuarterly.com*, June 2010.

represents more than 4,000 times the information stored in the U.S. Library of Congress.)[2] These networks form a global communications and information grid that enables large-scale interactions in an instant. Moreover, this expanding global grid is seeding new business models and accelerating the pace of innovation.

These two related developments—big data and the global grid—are combining to dramatically alter the role and mandate of procurement. During the next decade, the procurement function must better manage a wide range of issues raised by the quantum leap in information and connectivity: What are the most effective ways to combine diverse data to gain full visibility into the company's spend and supply base? How can advanced analytics be applied to understand and predict future demand for purchased products as well as cost and capacity development across the full value chain? How can procurement secure access to the latest innovations available in the supply market? How can CPOs use advanced technology to more effectively monitor the execution of sourcing strategies and track the benefits realized? How can new tools be used to negotiate most effectively in multivariable, multiconstraint scenarios? Are these unfamiliar fields of expertise for today's CPOs? For sure—but they are some that we believe CPOs have to explore to help their companies apply information and connectivity for competitive advantage.

New Insights and Collaboration at Scale Enhance Data-Driven Decisions

For businesses, big data and the global grid will have profound implications: they are enabling companies both to generate new insights and to collaborate at scale—which in turn allows them to raise data-driven decision making to a new level.

New Insights

Huge amounts of data are being stored and made available in electronic format. Examples are proliferating: the geospatial and geoeconomic data in Google Maps and Google Earth; the extensive profiles of millions of companies, both public and private, maintained by information services such as Dun & Bradstreet; and the consumer data aggregated by firms such as Nielsen. What's more, vast amounts of personal information are

---

[2]U.S. Library of Congress, accessed February 13, 2013, www.loc.gov/about/facts .html.

being posted and digitized on social media platforms. While much of this information was not intended for public dissemination, it too is snared in the web of big data and can be aggregated for commercial purposes. The enormous breadth, depth, and raw amount of data sets like these create opportunities to analyze multiple, dynamic variables. The ability to translate the trove of information into actionable insights will increasingly be a source of competitive advantage.

Collaboration at Scale

Information technology (IT)-enabled networking is rapidly increasing the speed of information flows, enabling the exchange of information around the globe at an ever-increasing pace. This has allowed companies to benefit from new levels of digital collaboration and cocreation within their networks, both internally and externally. The possibilities for collaboration have increased as the cost of bandwidth has declined; meanwhile, the overall capacity has increased and the evolution of mobile devices and network availability has improved the ease of connectivity. Ubiquitous bandwidth paired with massive central computing power has given rise to cloud computing. This technology enables individuals and institutions to leverage networks and central computing power to access and share data and software applications from any networked device across the world, further improving connectivity and collaboration.

By using technology to expand the scale and scope of collaboration, companies will be able to better integrate suppliers into processes from product design through customer fulfillment. Samsung, for example, like many high-tech companies, has opened up its web portals to hundreds of suppliers across the value chain.[3] Siemens collaborates virtually on its enterprise resource planning (ERP) network with a large number of its 40,000 suppliers.[4] Advanced sectors such as aerospace and automotive have been doing this for a decade by using proprietary EDI formats—but at substantial transaction costs. Now that digital connectivity and virtual collaboration are becoming more common among most domains (such as academia, government, and companies), adoption of virtual collaboration can be expected to accelerate quickly.

---

[3]"Sustainability," Samsung, accessed February 14, 2013, www.samsungsdi.com/ sustain/s2_5_1t.jsp.
[4]"Tools for Suppliers," Siemens, accessed February 14, 2013, https://w9.siemens.com/ cms/supply-chain-management/en/supplier-at-siemens/tools/Pages/tools.aspx.

Data-Driven Decision Making

With new insights and the ability to collaborate at scale, the potential of analytics to drive decision making has vastly increased. Existing analytics will be more informed and better executed; indeed, whole new categories of analysis will be possible. Imagine a procurement team so deeply connected into its suppliers that it gains access to all relevant data on cost structures, supply availability, lead times, and financial and operational risks, as well as service and quality metrics for its tier n supply base. Understanding these dimensions can lead to vastly improved, data-driven decision making. The procurement team would be well positioned to negotiate the right prices, instantaneously adapt its own planning, or switch to alternative suppliers in the case of supply shortages. It could even proactively help suppliers improve deteriorating quality levels by applying insights that are both deeper and surfaced earlier.

A Natural Role for Procurement

Procurement can play a significant role in a world where new insights from big data and collaboration at scale enable better, data-driven decision making.

Category managers and operational buyers sit at a crossroads of various data streams. Category managers first and foremost work with historical and future spending and usage data generated by the company's ERP and forecasting systems. They receive product specifications provided by their engineering counterparts and create comparative data, such as linear performance pricing or product-cost-driver analyses. Operational buyers monitor contract adherence, invoicing behavior, and supplier performance and generate supplier profiles and scorecards. All of these data are generated and processed by the company internally.

What's more, procurement is also tapping into various externally available data pools. To create category strategies, category managers access market data provided by external sources. They receive supply-market-specific time-series data for commodities, have access to currency and inflation rates, collect tax and tariff data, and even monitor weather developments using commercial information channels such as Bloomberg and Thomson Reuters. In specific areas, these information companies also provide real-time pricing, forecasts on pricing and supply, volatility analyses, and statistical comparisons. Beyond these traditional external sources, procurement is increasingly leveraging on-demand external specialist providers for information on financial assessments of current suppliers, forecasted market pricing, market supply-and-demand dynamics, and capacity status.

In addition to these external data providers, many procurement organizations have started to use procurement application software and services to assimilate and analyze data—either building the capabilities in-house or making use of firms such as Oracle, Ariba, and Global eProcure.

CPOs must recognize that they already possess a wealth of big data that can be converted into superior insights. Many of the data sources that sophisticated category managers are tapping today are not fully exploited, especially when it comes to combining different types of data and generating related insights. Starting with internal data, procurement could set up systematic dashboards to track, by department or unit, consumption levels in categories that include travel, facilities, postage, IT, and production materials. It could start continually augmenting these comparisons with externally generated benchmarks for the same KPIs.

Equally, through its work with these data streams, procurement sits at the crossroads of various internal and external relationships that may generate more value from better collaboration. By its very nature, procurement must engage with a broad spectrum of stakeholders, both inside and outside the organization. With regard to internal relationships, procurement leads the cross-functional category teams, involving all internal stakeholders from sales to manufacturing. And it is the company's representative to its external supply base, so it builds and maintains relationships with various stakeholders outside the company: current suppliers, prospective suppliers, regulators, customs and tax authorities, intellectual property or development partners, and the like.

Imagine how procurement could leverage both the data streams and the relationships it already possesses to play the end-to-end orchestrator role discussed in Chapter 4, "The Productivity Imperative: Orchestrating the End-to-End Value Chain." To make the orchestration vision a reality, procurement can connect various stakeholders along the value chain through, for example, digital collaboration platforms, shared data repositories, wikis, automatic dashboards, schedules, and escalation procedures.

As this discussion illustrates, procurement already owns many of the assets that it must leverage to play a larger role in the era of big data and the global grid. To fulfill this role, procurement must apply greater sophistication and entrepreneurship in exploiting existing data and relationships to create value for the company. Before we further explore the capabilities needed to achieve this step-up, we first consider the opportunities.

Opportunities in Core Procurement Activities, and Beyond

Leveraging new insights and collaboration at scale to advance data-driven decision making will create opportunities for procurement—both in enhancing its core activities as well as in expanding its mandate into areas beyond the core, such as risk management, innovation, and enterprise-wide coordination. The following ideas are intended to provide inspiration regarding the kinds of opportunities that we believe will become available in the future—and will even become commonly applied. Considering that the field of technology is probably the fastest moving of all the trends described in this book, we don't pretend to know what the future will look like with perfect clarity. But we want to use these ideas to trigger your thinking on what the opportunities could be.

Enhancing Procurement's Core Activities

Step-change improvements in core procurement activities will arise through enhanced negotiations and new opportunities in specification and in demand management. The following examples illustrate some of the ways that procurement can create additional value.

ENHANCED NEGOTIATION CAPABILITIES Good negotiators know that superior information is instrumental in any negotiation. Big data and advanced analytics help to improve negotiation intelligence, and they enable negotiators to model and play through more complex negotiation scenarios.

Heightened Negotiation Intelligence Data and insights are vital for successful negotiations. New insights driven by big data and advanced analytics can improve negotiation intelligence in many ways. The process starts with knowing which supplier to actually source from and negotiate with. The appropriate data regarding diverse supply markets, and connectivity into those markets, can help identify and prequalify potential suppliers in other regions, particularly low-cost countries (LCCs); the company can then use that information to prioritize suppliers to explore and work with. Having all the relevant negotiation arguments and insights readily prepared for a negotiation—including historical spending and savings patterns, market price developments for raw materials, supplier utilization information, and price comparisons and benchmarks—is the next step in adding value. Understanding the true "should cost" of the materials and services to buy is another insight that can be used both to set appropriate target prices (without losing credibility with the supplier as a result of non-fact-based, unrealistic requests) and to facilitate a discussion of supplier cost structures and margins, thereby ensuring that appropriate margins are secured. "Clean sheet" cost calculations can be applied to aid this effort. These are comprehensive, bottom-up "should cost" models that incorporate data from numerous internal and external sources, often using a special software application connected to a cost database. Finally, superior insights into the market dynamics of volatile commodities and energy can be used to develop analytical solutions for hedging and determining the right timing for purchases to be made.

Enhanced Negotiation Scenario Analyses As buying needs have become more complicated and modeling capabilities have grown more robust, procurement organizations are seizing opportunities to create value through enhanced negotiation scenario analyses. Scenario analysis involves designing models that calculate the impact of changes in the market, pricing, and availability of specific suppliers. Sophisticated multivariable scenarios can provide a step-change in modeling optimal outcomes on the basis of such parameters as unit price, shipping costs, and payment terms. These modeled outcomes can then be used to identify fully landed cost across a very high number of sources and users.

Consider a situation in which an organization seeks to make an informed purchase decision on a fleet of 20,000 vehicles, with seven vehicle types per region in 24 countries. Add to that mix 27 different cost elements with several suppliers bidding. Given the complexity of such scenarios and the risk of incorrect conclusions, leading organizations are already using advanced analytics supplied by third-party providers and specialists to navigate the data sets and identify the optimal scenario.

Another example is the sourcing of maintenance, repair, and operations (MRO). For most manufacturers, this commodity typically has more than 10,000 SKUs across multiple subcommodities such as safety items, consumables and lubricants, bearings and springs, and larger-ticket items such as motors and pumps. Frequently, sourcing decisions are determined by analyzing small subsets of the SKUs from each subcommodity and making extrapolations. Procurement can greatly improve sourcing decisions on MRO spending by applying advanced analyses to better understand demand from various users and their respective specifications, pricing levels from various suppliers, and supply constraints, as well as total cost of ownership (TCO) elements such as shipping costs.

Last, consider the example of an advanced hospital network in the United States that leverages physicians' utilization data to provide visibility into the medical devices and pharmaceuticals prescribed by individual physicians. The data complement traditional supplier and SKU spend data that are normally available to hospitals. The enhanced perspective on the physicians' consumption patterns provides insights and points of leverage when negotiating with device manufacturers and pharmaceutical firms, which lack insights into buying behavior, local demand trends, and available substitutes and savings potentials. This example offers another potential benefit not directly linked to supply chain optimization: physicians' utilization data can be linked to patients, enabling the application of advanced analytics based on disease state and providing a fact base with which to better manage treatment outcomes.

BETTER MANAGEMENT OF SPECIFICATIONS AND DEMAND Leading procurement organizations have long been applying data to reduce the consumption and quantity of various inputs and thereby to better manage specifications and demand. The advent of big data and the global grid is, however, driving significantly enhanced and new opportunities.

Understanding True Demand Real-time understanding of demand patterns and trends, enabled by better connectivity and increased data exchange, allows procurement teams to better determine which goods and services to buy, in what quantity, and at what time. Consider enhanced forecasting abilities that use multiple customer, market, competitor, and supplier inputs to arrive at better estimates of future sales, and consequently determine requirements for sourced raw materials, parts, and services. The value of enhanced forecasting can be captured through the avoidance of purchasing too much of a given commodity, or buying too little and then paying premiums for expedited delivery or a higher cost due to rising market prices. Additionally, more and better data can improve decisions relating to both the timing and the type of purchases of large capital assets such as ships and airplanes. The available shipping tonnage capacity in the market, for example, significantly drives the purchase price; with insight into this capacity, a purchaser can better determine whether to buy new or used assets.

As another example, analyzing digital media spend to uncover consumers' buying patterns can yield significant insights to shape negotiations and media purchases. The insights might allow the company to allocate its media spend to specific days, times, or online channels with higher return on investment (ROI).

Understanding the true demand also covers any supplementary sources of demand, such as logistics, packaging, and maintenance, that are typically captured in TCO considerations. In the future, comprehensive TCO models will be built dynamically from various input data available in the grid.

Benchmarking Demand and Specification Levels As indicated earlier, procurement organizations can help establish far-reaching KPI systems to benchmark indirect spend by the business, by business units, and even by budget owners, on a category-by-category level. In travel, for example, KPIs that measure spend per employee can be augmented with operational KPIs such as travel bookings made a minimum of 10 days in advance or for business versus economy class. Many of these KPIs will become more comparable across different companies, allowing for cross-company and cross-industry benchmarks.

Ultimately, these benchmarks can inform new policies. Organizations are leveraging behavioral data to design policies that impose restrictions on purchase types or volume. Understanding precise usage patterns for certain software applications, data terminals, or room occupations can trigger changes in the specific provisioning to individual employees or groups or even to company spending policies as a whole. One multinational company, for example, recently analyzed its parcel and air-freight spend across dozens of shipping modes, hundreds of sites, and tens of millions of shipments. The analysis suggested that tightening simple rules—such as prohibiting express freight shipments on Fridays and mandating the use of the least expensive vendor per route—could yield U.S. $28 million in annual savings.

Ensuring Compliance Big data and the global grid can also help with new policies that require mechanisms to secure compliance. Most important is the ability to dynamically track transactional buying activities wherever and whenever they occur; another key area is implementation of gating mechanisms for purchase orders and invoices, such as requiring a purchase order for payments and prohibiting backdating.

In addition to these opportunities in strategic negotiation and specification and in demand management, there are, of course, many other benefits from big data and the global grid with respect to operational and tactical procurement. Here, most benefits come from connecting with suppliers more efficiently, gathering relevant information such as shipping or payment data, or allowing more seamless interactions. Increasing automation levels in both operational and strategic sourcing activities can create benefits, at minimum by freeing up procurement personnel for activities that add greater value.

Increasing Value Beyond Traditional Procurement Activities

Big data and the global grid will also allow procurement to extend its area of influence beyond its core activities and thus to add more value to other functions and the business at large. Procurement's ability to do so rests on its elevated position at the crossroads of various data streams and relationships, as described previously.

CROSS-SECTOR CONSORTIUM BUYING Purchasing through volume is a well-established concept by which companies consolidate expenditures across business units to maximize their negotiating leverage with suppliers. Big data and advanced analytics will allow companies to raise these efforts to a new level by enabling companies to come together and purchase supplies across industries as a consortium. The consortia can apply supply market and sourcing data analysis to bundle their procurement spend on direct raw material and thereby capture synergies and discounts from aggregated volume commitments.

External providers can help individual companies execute this approach to consortium buying. One specialist firm helps process more than U.S. $100 billion of raw materials purchasing annually in such industries as oil and chemicals. As another example, industrial companies located in close proximity can pool their purchasing power to cooperate on purchases for raw materials such as steel, aluminum, or glass.

TIME-TO-MARKET INITIATIVES Data sources and online connectivity are also enabling continual collaboration that allows companies to reduce the time to market for new products. The aerospace industry provides striking examples. For instance, over the past 15 years, the time to market has shrunk from 25 years for the Boeing 747 to 12 years for the Airbus A380, primarily as a result of two factors: virtual product design and testing, which have been accelerated significantly through the use of portals that transfer data in real time between Airbus and its extensive supply base, and advanced analytics that leverage large data sets. The retail and electronics industries are also speeding products to market through connectivity and institutionalizing collaboration within information and data domains. This has enabled these organizations to reduce the time to market for laptops, flat-screen TVs, and other such products to levels previously considered impossible.

RISK AND COMPLIANCE MANAGEMENT Going forward, procurement will play a much larger role in risk management, as we discuss in Chapter 6, "Volatility as the New Normal: Translating Sourcing Risk into Competitive Advantage." At the basic level of risk management, procurement can leverage external providers to monitor the financial status of existing strategic suppliers, identify any changes, and determine whether and how to switch suppliers before the supply chain can be interrupted.

In the United States, the recent implementation of many new and complicated regulations for financial services is affecting nearly all businesses operating in this field. And the regulations affect nearly all functions: From a procurement point of view, regulatory issues arise in the management of vendors, which financial institutions use for traditional services such as IT and marketing, for instance. Additional issues relate to navigating the use of mandated external providers for auditing services. Consider the billions of transactions annually that contain confidential consumer information. External parties execute many of the automated processes, which puts procurement in charge of establishing systems to ensure that confidentiality requirements are met at all times.

INNOVATION Procurement will also be able to add value in the area of direct intellectual property and innovation. In the pharmaceutical industry, large players are investing more resources to acquire patent rights or the smaller biotech start-ups that control those rights, after clinical trials have advanced to a certain stage. Many marketplaces have already piloted the sale of patented innovation. Marketplaces for unpatented and unprotected knowledge are likely to develop as the transition to open-source innovation continues. Procurement can play a role by scouting these new patents, applications, and technologies; to do so, procurement organizations must connect deeply into these networks and develop the skills to assess, source, and advance innovations, working together with internal R&D departments.

MONETIZATION OF PROPRIETARY INFORMATION Generating revenues by offering insights derived from internal proprietary information, either alone or in combination with external sources, is potentially another source of value creation. We already described how certain hospitals leverage usage-pattern data in negotiations with medical device and pharmaceutical manufacturers. Selling the same type of data, potentially enhanced by actionable insights, is one example of how the procurement organization can monetize acquired data.

Procurement also has opportunities to work with other functions within the company to provide integrated data and insights that are valuable to suppliers and other third parties. Manufacturers in the automotive, rail, and heavy equipment sectors, for example, possess an abundance of data about overall product quality, failures, and maintenance. Typically, they are the hub that receives this information from customers and dealers. Integrated data from manufacturers that enables a better understanding of the causes of failure and specific breakdowns can be of immense value to the suppliers of parts and assemblies. These data sets from manufacturers are often much more comprehensive than any internal data the suppliers could generate themselves. The manufacturer can leverage these data for commercial benefit in the form of direct credit for future purchases or direct generation of revenues. Although the procurement function doesn't necessarily own warranty data from dealers, it can play a central role in consolidating and leveraging such data for suppliers.

Capabilities to Capture the Opportunities

Many procurement organizations will have to build significant capabilities in various areas in order to capture opportunities such as those described earlier in this chapter. During the past few years, many procurement functions have devoted significant time and resources to building e-procurement tools, including eRFX, eAuctions, spending cubes, and performance- and knowledge-management systems. In fact, our Global Purchasing Excellence (GPE) survey confirmed the high correlation between strong global procurement organizations and their knowledge management systems. Our GPE research found that strong global procurement organizations are six times more likely to have strong and well-organized knowledge management systems. Overall, however, "knowledge and information management" scored the lowest among all assessment dimensions in the survey.

To define an agenda for capturing value from big data and the global grid, CPOs should first thoroughly assess where the greatest value will be found, in both the short term and the long term. Many organizations will have to start by cleaning up their basic spend transparency and management systems and establishing internal spend KPIs. Others may be able to build on existing data and analytics kernels in procurement or other functions to target specific areas of additional value creation, as explored earlier.

In any case, CPOs should consider their entrepreneurial journey into big data as one with two legs: building the foundation, and then expanding and piloting the effort to build credibility.

Building the Foundation

The ability to capture value from big data and the global grid rests on a foundation of analytical talent and technical solutions. In some cases, the talent and solutions may already reside in-house; in other cases, the company will need to turn to the external market.

BUILD AN ANALYTICAL TALENT PIPELINE Practitioners will need the individual and collective skills required to drive forward procurement's big data and advanced analytics. The primary skill set will be analytical aptitude—the ability to quickly develop early hypotheses on the opportunities and then effectively structure, synthesize, and interpret relevant internal and external data to glean meaningful insights. In many cases, this will require significant creativity and problem-solving capabilities. Because promising areas for insights and impact may not always be fully and immediately obvious, practitioners must recognize the need to persevere and, over time, develop the skills to properly read and judge the signals from the data and to iteratively probe deeper.

Furthermore, these practitioners will need the analytical dexterity to identify how they can use the new wealth of information to address fundamentally different possibilities and questions. Savvy practitioners will be able to spot other innovative opportunities that would add substantial value for the company. Practitioners also need to understand how concepts can be transferred among sectors or commodities and how to apply and extract similar insights in other areas.

How can procurement acquire and develop this talent? When recruiting externally, procurement must strike a capability balance between high analytical aptitude and core procurement and commodity experience. Many high-performing procurement organizations wisely look for applicants with analytics capabilities and then train the new hires in functional procurement skills. The business and science programs of top academic institutions are often incubators of the required expertise in both analytics and problem solving.

Talent development should include training on tools and techniques specific to procurement analytics, including granular spend analytics, RFQ analysis, and potentially several tools customized to individual companies.

SOURCE OR DEVELOP TECHNICAL SOLUTIONS TO ANALYZE BIG DATA Procurement functions will, in effect, be placing bets on select technical solutions and tools to capture first-mover advantage; they will be the early adopters of potentially transformative solutions. Consequently, the first generation of practitioners also need to be adept at scouting out and assessing new technologies, techniques, and services that can drive meaningful insights at optimal speed and cost.

Many new analytics will require new types of tools and software applications, beyond the classical tools (Microsoft Excel and Access, spend-cube systems, and the like). The procurement function will need to decide which analytical tools or data warehouses and services are best suited to be sourced externally from specialist providers or developed internally. Fortunately, the mainstreaming of big data is also driving the development of purpose-built analytical tools to process big data, and external service providers of on-demand solutions are proliferating. The scope and scale of these firms can be expected to increase significantly in the next decade. Procurement organizations need to be correspondingly flexible in working with smaller, early-stage firms that are pushing the frontiers of analytics but may not yet have established track records. Procurement must also determine how to deal with confidentiality and intellectual property rights when consolidating data from various sources into central data warehouses for analysis. This will require procurement to work with IT and legal departments to introduce mechanisms to prevent and track the specific usage of information.

Because many of these new tools are only now emerging, solutions will initially be quite tailored to the specific value-creation areas in which they are applied. Procurement practitioners should be prepared to take a trial-and-error approach, and be intensively involved in the design or customizing of any solution. And, because today's leading-edge solution may be only on par—if not outdated—in a short time, practitioners will need to engage with the vendor market regularly and be an early adopter in select areas. This will also give them a strong voice in driving later decisions regarding which technical solutions to employ in the longer run.

Targeted Expansion and Pilots

Big data and advanced analytics solutions should be practical and focused on adding value. The greatest initial value, for example, may be found in fixing basic spend transparency issues or helping manufacturing get better and deeper insights into the key metrics of suppliers that ultimately influence their own factory performance. Success entails focusing on select high-value topics, closely aligning with key stakeholders and gaining their support, and delivering insights and value quickly.

GAIN CREDIBILITY In parallel, initial measures should be taken to communicate the ways in which procurement can provide more valuable, data-driven perspectives. To gain credibility, it will be critical to involve analytical practitioners in situations and committees in which they can share the insights they've generated. This might include having a place on the corporate risk committee, so that procurement can share insights about specific geographies or commodities critical to the supply chain. It might also entail participating in strategic planning to showcase some of the latest scenario modeling on the range of outcomes for upcoming sourcing events, or larger issues such as how various future market prices would impact earnings before interest, taxes, depreciation, and amortization (EBITDA). These changes won't happen overnight; they will result only from deliberate efforts and placements.

DRAW LESSONS FROM PILOTS Procurement should draw lessons from pilot projects and elevate promising experiments to a higher level. These lessons would relate to, for example, the quality of analysis and insights, the speed and cost of securing information and making decisions, and the organization's readiness to embrace new solutions and insights. Practitioners should also seek to identify which solutions are specific to particular areas and which are sufficiently general that they can be applied to other areas. While advanced spending-cube solutions and usage KPIs may be applicable across virtually all categories, in-depth analysis and operational perspectives into the supply chain down to tier n may be relevant for only a few critical suppliers and items. This is also true for sophisticated risk-management services to prevent supply interruptions; for certain commodities, the impact of a supply chain interruption could be millions of dollars per day in revenue losses that could be prevented through decision making and planning that are supported by advanced analytics, whereas for other commodities, readily available substitutes may allow companies to focus only on the need for prompt action.

CREATE VALUE BY EXPANDING THE PILOTS To target the expansion of pilot areas, procurement must understand where additional value resides. Often, existing pilot projects can be expanded into adjacent areas, covering additional categories, suppliers, or metrics. Success and sustainability at the enterprise level requires orchestrated communication and syndication from the original pilots. Additionally, successful practitioners who distinguish themselves as change agents in the pilot projects should be elevated to prominent leadership roles in business units, finance, risk management, and corporate strategy, as well as senior procurement roles. Scaling up will also require changes to tools and/or processes, such as the approach to identifying and qualifying external providers of analytics or information services. Furthermore, the company must determine when to begin migrating from systems developed in-house to service-on-demand models from external providers. It must also decide on the right time to redeploy analytics practitioners to new, cutting-edge topics. To do this effectively, practitioners should assess the performance and ROI of specific initiatives undertaken, including developing an after-action analysis approach to reflect on the quality of insights generated.

■ ■ ■

During the next decade, big data and the global grid will combine to enable new levels of control, collaboration, and value extraction. To leverage the opportunities arising, procurement must seek to become:

- The trusted consolidator and owner of all data exchanged at the company's interface with its supply base.
- A master in structuring, synthesizing, interpreting, and applying the abundance of data on markets and suppliers to decision-making problems.
- An intrepid explorer of new types of analytics that convert supply-base-related big data into new opportunities.
- An early adopter of new technologies and a codeveloper of new analytical tools and solutions that can generate value.

Procurement's ability to successfully leverage big data and the global grid to create value will be critical to the company's efforts to manage risk in the increasingly volatile global business environment. The next chapter, "Volatility as the New Normal: Translating Sourcing Risk into Competitive Advantage," discusses how procurement must become agile to adapt to an environment of impermanence and ever-faster change.

Volatility as the New Normal: Translating Sourcing Risk into Competitive Advantage

Main Messages

- Procurement will have to manage not only the increasing scarcity of raw materials but also substantially greater volatility that will have a significant impact on a company's profitability and ability to do business.
- Defensive strategies, such as hedging or recovery plans, will be part of the solution, but not all of it.
- Agile procurement will allow CPOs to cope with risks; doing this well will also allow them to capture opportunities and create a competitive advantage by better managing sourcing risks.

In the past, procurement operated within the relatively stable parameters of rising commodity prices, albeit with some discrete discontinuities. This environment is changing, however, and will continue to evolve in the coming years. It is being replaced not so much by new ground rules as by persistent uncertainty. Early warning signs are apparent. As global demand for natural resources and commodities increases, so does the risk of supply chain disruptions.

Consider Honda. While the carmaker's weighted raw-material index increased by more than 200 percent between 2009 and 2012, the average prices for its cars remained stable. Honda was also hurt in 2011 by the earthquake and tsunami in Japan and floods in Thailand; production facilities located in these regions were hit hard. The carmaker lost sales of 260,000 vehicles as a consequence of the floods alone, resulting in a 59 percent reduction in net profit.[1] In addition, lanthanum, a key commodity used for hybrid car batteries, is beyond the edge of scarcity[2]—demand is higher than supply. Both the volatility of the marketplace and the scarcity of materials are destined to become major concerns, and they underscore the need for a new approach to procurement. It is reasonable to expect that in the near future the combination of protectionism, an increasing global population, and the rising standard of living in emerging economies will stretch supply chains dangerously taut.

Traditional best practices as described in Chapter 1, "The Drivers of Sustainable Procurement Performance," provide a solid foundation from which to build, but considerably more effort and innovation will be required in the future. Risk management has already established itself as a key differentiator between procurement leaders and followers, as our Global Purchasing Excellence (GPE) research suggests. But the prerequisites to risk management will change in the future, and key competencies regarding how companies manage volatility and scarcity will distinguish those who succeed. CPOs and their teams, as the natural owners of risk management, will play a pivotal role in coordinating the required cross-functional preemptive responses. In the same way that risk management is reconceptualized in ISO 31000[3] from a defensive posture to an offensive opportunity to create value, so too will procurement need to evolve.

But how can procurement assume this offensive role? In other words, how can procurement organizations become supply entrepreneurs? What are leading organizations already doing to protect against—or even gain advantage from—the rising volatility? What distinguishes companies in which procurement is recognized as the gatekeeper of the company's access to resources and is included in decisions regarding product design and development? What sophisticated tools are they leveraging for both financial and physical risk management? How do they make manufacturing more flexible to increase production during peak times with dedicated

---

[1]Mircea Serafim, "Thai Floods: Honda Lost 260,000 Cars," *Inautonews*, January 31, 2012, www.inautonews.com/thai-floods-honda-lost-260000-cars#.UR5iex2kp5c.

[2]Ian Cooper, "Dangerous Rare Earth Supply Risk," *Wealth Daily*, December 29, 2011, www.wealthdaily.com/articles/dangerous-rare-earth-supply-risk/3351.

[3]ISO 31000 seeks to provide a universally recognized paradigm for practitioners and companies employing risk management processes to replace the myriad of existing standards, methodologies, and paradigms that have differed between industries, subject matters, and regions.

suppliers? And how do they become more deeply networked and embedded in global sourcing markets to gain vital foresight into volatility?

CPOs and their procurement organizations will have to cope with this new era of volatility by becoming agile—adapting their buying behavior, rhythm, contracts, and hedging strategies to an environment of impermanence and ever-faster change.

An Era of Greater Volatility

A variety of measures suggest that business has entered an economic era characterized by both higher commodity prices and higher upstream volatility.

Commodity prices have significantly increased since the turn of this century, erasing in a decade all of the price declines that occurred during the 1900s; the McKinsey Global Institute (MGI) commodity index, which had dropped approximately 80 percent between 1900 and 1999, has more than doubled since 2000 (see Exhibit 6.1).[4] Moreover, the upward slope is growing steeper.

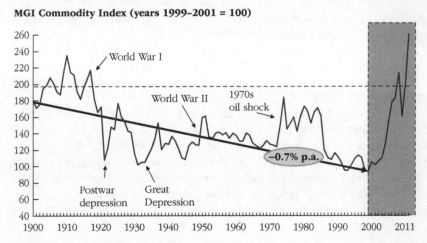

MGI Commodity Index (years 1999–2001 = 100)

EXHIBIT 6.1 Commodity Prices, 1900–2011. Since the turn of this century, commodity prices have significantly increased, eroding all of the price falls seen since 1900

Source: McKinsey Global Institute.

---

[4]McKinsey analysis.

Comparing the volatility rates of 1997–2007 with those of 2008–2011 reveals that the volatility of corn prices rose 58 percent in the latter period, wheat rose 61 percent, and soy 54 percent. Among materials, crude prices increased in volatility by 10 percent, copper by 50 percent, and aluminum by 75 percent.[5] The significant correlation existing between commodity volatility and oil prices, which began to appear in 2000, has strengthened since 2005.[6]

Some industries—for instance, airlines, which are highly dependent on kerosene prices—already have considerable experience dealing with extreme price volatility. Lufthansa, for example, had to pay €1 billion more for fuel in 2012 compared with 2011.[7] But for many others, this extreme volatility is new territory. For a consumer goods company like Henkel, raw-material costs as a percentage of sales grew by 22 percent from 2007 through 2011.[8] Although the intensity of such broad volatility may be new for some companies, others have already experienced the pain of being on the wrong side of a price swing. One major automotive original equipment manufacturer (OEM), for example, posted a $1 billion loss on palladium and other precious metals contracts in 2001, causing shareholders to file suits alleging mistakes in the company's hedging practices.

Worldwide demand for resources is increasing, notably because emerging markets are becoming richer. This will make resources even more scarce. For example, our MGI research has found that known iron reserves are expected to decline by 2 percent annually, putting pressure on steel and other metals. The world's need for energy will require that 70 percent more energy be generated by 2030. Demand for food will double over the same period. Across a whole range of commodities and raw materials, purchasing will have to cope with potential scarcity and volatility.

Meanwhile, the incidence and impact of disruptive natural disasters have increased of late, another factor contributing to volatility. Five of the 10 costliest natural disasters in history occurred in the past four years; reinsurer Munich Re estimates that resulting economic costs in 2011 reached a record $378 billion. Sony posted a net loss for fiscal year 2011 of ¥520 billion, resulting among other reasons from the lingering effects of damage from the tsunami in Japan and flooding in its Thailand

---

[5]McKinsey analysis.

[6]McKinsey analysis.

[7]"High Fuel Costs and Air Traffic Tax Burden Lufthansa Result for 2011," Lufthansa, accessed February 25, 2013, www.lufthansagroup.com/en/press/news-releases/singleview/archive/2012/march/15/article/2101.html.

[8]McKinsey analysis.

manufacturing hub.[9] "Whether the economic toll of disasters is rising faster than global GDP is unclear, since a wealthier world naturally has more wealth at risk," observed *The Economist*. "Still, the incidence of spectacular, multi-billion-dollar catastrophes seems certain to rise."[10] This is also caused by more intense economic activities occurring in high-risk geographical regions—like the Japanese coastline.

While CPOs and other operations executives face volatility every day from major disruptions and normal operational variability, they are often inadequately prepared to effectively manage their high-priority risks. For example, on a scale of 0 (very well prepared) to 10 (completely unprepared), they rated an average of 7 with regard to addressing the risk of supplier insolvencies. Executives feel significantly unprepared in such areas as demand volatility, supplier insolvencies, and currency volatility. And while disruptive events have not been occurring more frequently, the global interconnectivity of supply chains has increased their impact.

The New Model of Agile Procurement

To cope with volatility as it becomes the new normal, the procurement function must become more responsive to more factors than ever before. In a word, it must become agile. Agile procurement has a measurable benefit, and entails decision making that is both strategic (where and how to build agility) as well as operational (which specific levers to pull). As long as reducing costs remained the most important concern of procurement managers, agility was more or less synonymous with improved forecast accuracy. But now that procurement's priority is shifting to management of volatility, scarcity, and disruptions, forecasting alone is not enough. To become truly agile, procurement must expand its approach to consider other elements of agility, such as anticipation, reaction time, and cross-functionality.

Anticipation

Wal-Mart provides an example of one element of agility: the ability to anticipate change. In 2002, 29 ports on the West Coast of the United States were closed when a breakdown in labor negotiations resulted in a strike. All material flow through the ports was halted and hundreds of cargo-bearing ships were stranded at sea for 10 days until the federal

---

[9]"Sony Revises Expected Loss to $6.4 billion," *New York Times*, April 10, 2012.

[10]"Counting the Cost of Calamities," *Economist*, January 14, 2012.

government intervened. The estimated impact of the shutdown was U.S. $20 billion. Many companies suffered weeks of delays while the backlog of stranded ships was processed through the ports. Wal-Mart, which had been closely watching the progress of the labor negotiations, was one of only a few companies to anticipate the strike and port closure. It used airfreight to preemptively built inventory and protect its supply of goods before the shutdown occurred.[11]

What are the five key risks for your institution? How forward-looking is your perspective on procurement? Agile procurement looks for and anticipates uncertainty, rather than just managing the current environment. Leaders know their relevant risk types and have assigned a monetary value to them. And they proactively mitigate these risks. Taking this forward-looking perspective entails, for example, the ongoing monitoring of key metrics that measure a supplier's health. It also means identifying an alternative supplier that can be called upon quickly if the original supplier's risk profile becomes excessive.

For example, a global aircraft builder monitors all of its suppliers with respect to risk—even as far downstream as tier 3 and tier 4. The company has dual sourcing for all key components, even though this reduces leveraging opportunities in contracting. Plus, it knows where its suppliers are located. In contrast, many automotive OEMs were surprised to learn that they were affected by the Fukushima disaster because of exposure to lower-tier suppliers they didn't know about. As their experience shows, buying practices intended to optimize relationships with only key suppliers come at a hidden price. By overconsolidating suppliers without closely monitoring them, companies lose the ability to achieve high levels of flexibility in sourcing. In an era of greater volatility, this is a prescription for risk. One of the leading global auto OEMs suffered severely when the single-source supplier of door keys—a relative commodity—stopped deliveries, thereby causing significant production shortages.

Time

When a hurricane destroyed 80 percent of the banana crop in Honduras, the revenues of two major global fruit traders were affected differently. One of the companies lost 70 percent of its supply—and revenues fell by 4 percent because it could not replace the lost bananas. The other company also lost its supply in Honduras but was able to increase output from

---

[11]J. Schmitt, "Using Stochastic Supply Inventory Models to Strategically Mitigate Supply Chain Disruption Risk," *Logistics Spectrum*, 2008; "Managing Supply-Chain Risk for Reward," *Economist Intelligence Unit*, 2009.

alternative suppliers in unaffected areas—enabling it to increase revenues by 4 percent.[12]

After an incident disrupts supply, leading companies aren't simply faster than the competition at getting back to normal. They also find ways to use time as a competitive advantage. Being able to react faster than the competition to uncertainties, and thereby gain advantages in cost and market share, will become an increasingly important differentiator. A company that can recover from an earthquake faster by using a more flexible supplier footprint than the competition, for example, will position itself to capture market share. One of the world's largest amusement park operators has contracts with temporary labor providers that allow it to adjust staffing on an hourly schedule based on the weather.

Cross-Functionality

At one of the leading global manufacturers of flavors and juices, no sales contract is signed until procurement has reviewed the raw-material assumptions made in the calculation. At a global chewing-gum manufacturer, procurement works with the marketing function to decide what particular products to promote at particular times on the basis of raw-material price inputs—in the same way that restaurants select the soup of the day. The CPO of a leading global food company is actively involved in initiating changes in product recipes. The company changes the formulation of its margarine products on the basis of the price levels of raw materials for vegetable oil.

What is your level of influence outside of procurement? How often do you meet with your peers from sales and R&D? CPOs should consider ways to gain the benefits of these cross-functional initiatives. Agile procurement goes beyond six sigma by instituting a truly cross-functional effort that takes a forward-looking view and embraces uncertainties that may ultimately affect processes and performance. Volume volatility, for example, should be considered in system design through cross-training of the workforce, the use of temporary workers, and requiring flexible supplier contracts.

Comprehensive View

One global metals company was able to effectively manage a shortage of key materials, whereas a competitor had to stop production. Prior to the disruption, the successful company had institutionalized collaboration

---

[12]Ibid.

between procurement and manufacturing so that source material could be used in a wider range of quality grades without affecting the finished product's performance. Preemptive levers were introduced, including flexible contracts that allowed for adjustments in volumes purchased from individual vendors and vendor sites, investments in internal production capacity that allowed for the blending of lower-quality materials from marginal players as extenders, and the introduction of a supplier development program to coach suppliers on how to change their refining processes to produce the optimal grade for any given plant.

To improve its detection and response capabilities, the company had established market intelligence teams in each region. These teams were responsible for developing an informed point of view about likely changes to the price and availability of commodities, the drivers for those changes, and the implications for the specific business. These were used to drive purchasing behavior and contract formation and were embedded into forward-looking business plans. A central group of highly skilled managers and analysts provided support to the individual business units, reviewing all contracts above a defined threshold, performing scenario analysis on what could go wrong, and suggesting appropriate mitigation strategies.

Does your team follow the example of this metals company in taking a fully comprehensive view on volatility and preparing a holistic means of dealing with it? A survey published by the logistics firm DHL[13] in 2012 reported that 23 percent of large companies did not include their entire supply chain in their business continuity plan. Disaster risk management may provide false comfort if it stops at the enterprise's walls and does not include upstream suppliers, for example. Agile procurement goes beyond lean by considering longer time periods, and thereby provides a more complete view of how volatility changes the return on the flexibility that savvy investments in the supply base provide. Whereas the traditional business case for flexible assets considers the likely volatility of demand based on historical data, true agility requires looking ahead to the future volatility of supply.

It is clear in these examples that companies seeking to benefit from volatility are enhancing the function of procurement and the role of the CPO. They are recognizing that procurement is an early sensor of volatility and, through its reactions, is the supply chain's preemptive risk manager. Moreover, procurement is uniquely positioned to add value by seizing opportunities presented by volatility. The procurement function is

---

[13]"Supply Chain Resilience 2011," *Business Continuity Institute*, accessed March 12, 2013, www.zurichna.com/internet/zna/sitecollectiondocuments/en/corporatebusiness/riskengineering/supply_chain_resilience_2011.pdf.

also pivotal as a source of data—leveraging tools and systems as described in Chapter 5, "Big Data and the Global Grid: Procurement's New Role in Data-Driven Decision Making"—and analytical capabilities. In many companies, it is also the coordinator of relevant cross-functional actions.

Consequently, CPOs must look beyond the capabilities required to execute purchasing in an ever-fluid resource environment to consider how they can play a leading role in aligning procurement with corporate strategy. Combining these two general functions—purchasing and alignment—constitutes the next stage in procurement agility.

How to Think about Creating Preemptive Agility

Preemptive agility levers are put in place before a disruptive event occurs. These preparatory initiatives are intended to reduce the likely impact of uncertainty on the organization or to improve the organization's future ability to respond. CPOs can incorporate a variety of perspectives as they create preemptive agility for the procurement function.

Factoring Uncertainties into the Supply Base of the Future

Factoring uncertainties into supplier strategy decisions builds agile procurement into the whole supplier life cycle. Procurement leaders of the future will measure uncertainty through quantitative analyses, modeling scenarios to take key uncertainties, such as supplier bankruptcy or material scarcity, into account. They will then define strategies and design a supplier portfolio based on expected values (prices and costs) rather than those defined in contracts. They will always have alternative solutions ready to be activated for critical suppliers and parts. They will consider the overall, global supplier footprint, and they will evaluate and compare all possible supply solutions: make versus buy, backward integration versus direct sourcing options, and single versus multiple sourcing.

Li & Fung is an example of a company that factors uncertainty into its supplier strategy. As the largest outsourcing agent in the apparel industry, having $10 billion in revenues and 12,000 suppliers in more than 20 countries, it was particularly vulnerable to volatility. It now has the ability to instantly switch to alternative suppliers and countries to minimize exposure to currency risk, quota and tariff risks, raw-material price risks, political risks, and other risks.[14]

As another example, a global tire manufacturer reduced costs by 7 percent through global dynamic sourcing of polybutadiene rubber. The

---

[14]McKinsey analysis.

company made arbitrage gains by switching sourcing regions when appropriate. This was enabled by building up suppliers in all regions and by contracting in a way that allows the manufacturer to switch among them.

To secure its supply of lanthanum, a rare earth element, Toyota has become the first and only car company to invest in a rare earth mine. First discovered in 1893, lanthanum is more abundant than silver or lead and is the second most abundant rare earth element. Because there weren't significant uses for it, though, lanthanum mostly went into stockpile, waiting for the day when it could be sold off for higher prices. That day has come. Today, every Toyota Prius hybrid car carries about 10 pounds of lanthanum as the metal in its nickel-metal hydride battery.[15] These batteries pack more power into a smaller space—they're about twice as efficient as the standard lead-acid car battery. Lanthanum's general abundance aside, there is not enough of it available on the supply market today to meet demand for this breakthrough technology, which is also used in other hybrid cars and small mopeds in China.

Helix, a maker of high-performance vacuum pumps, illustrates the flexible supplier approach with its "demand flow technology," an operational strategy version of lean that enables it to segment manufacturing processes into short, easily taught subprocesses.[16] In the event of a disruption in a Helix plant, these subprocesses can be quickly taught to suppliers so that they can make the company's products. This requires Helix to analyze the capacity and capabilities of its suppliers, and to enter into flexible volume contracts with them. More than 3,200 companies use Helix's demand flow technology, including GE and Boeing.

Developing Suppliers and Their Ecosystems

Building agile suppliers and investing in their ecosystems will have a lasting impact on supply stability and quality. Future leaders will include risk preparedness as a key dimension in the criteria for supplier selection. They will correspondingly support suppliers with agility best practices and collaboratively develop an integrated approach to risk management by sharing know-how, investing in training suppliers, holding joint workshops, and defining shared risk-management standards.

---

[15]"Rare Earth Elements That Will Only Get More Important," *Popular Mechanics*, accessed March 13, 2013, www.popularmechanics.com/technology/engineering/news/important-rare-earth-elements#slide-1.

[16]Yossi Sheffi, *The Resilient Enterprise: Overcoming Vulnerability for Competitive Advantage* (Cambridge, MA: MIT Press, 2005).

To sustain an agile network, they will adopt a more structured, standardized approach to selecting and approving new suppliers in markets experiencing temporary volatility. They will also invest directly in the development of the supplier ecosystem (see Chapter 7, "The New Economic Drivers: Capturing the Total Impact of Environmental, Social, and Regulatory Factors") by cooperating with local authorities, investing in stabilization and development funds, and lobbying.

Diageo, Ikea, and Nestlé are companies that develop agile suppliers.[17]

Diageo invests in farmer development in Kenya, providing technical training to more than 10,000 farmers to ensure quality. Supply security goes hand in hand with lower cost of goods sold (COGS), because it decreases the need to import more expensive barley and enables reduced shipping costs. This allows Diageo to ensure supply as well as to hedge prices and mitigate risk. Similar programs have already been implemented in Nigeria, Ghana, Sierra Leone, and Cameroon.

Ikea is fully financing training small-hold cotton farmers in India and Pakistan. The training for better cotton cultivation is conducted by the World Wildlife Fund (WWF) and supervised by Ikea employees. The effort has involved more than 18,000 farmers, who can produce a cumulative capacity of 150,000 metric tons. Farmers save 4 to 7 percent of their input costs. Use of water has been reduced by 50 percent, pesticides by more than 50 percent, and chemical fertilizers by more than 35 percent.

Nestlé tackles volatility and ensures the quality of milk by establishing long-term relationships with thousands of Chinese suppliers. The company buys fresh milk from some 25,000 Chinese dairy farmers and provides the group with an overall income of approximately 500,000 Swiss francs per day. Nestlé has also undertaken several initiatives to establish deeper relationships with farmers. It helps to arrange affordable bank loans for farmers so that they can expand their capacity, and it has helped to find local suppliers for essential equipment. Nestlé is seeking to reduce the cost of feed by enabling farmers to deal directly with suppliers rather than having to go through an intermediary. To help farmers improve their capabilities, the company has arranged for advice and visits from agronomists. All of this also helps Nestlé to track quality control more closely.

Building Flexibility into Supplier and Customer Contracting Strategies

Future leaders will create volume and price flexibility with suppliers through robust and transparent contracting strategies. They will limit

---

[17]McKinsey analysis on public company information.

exposure to market fluctuations with their suppliers through staggered and flexible volume contracts. If they are in a strong-enough position, the easiest way for companies to handle volatility is simply to pass their costs on to customers.

Financial hedging instruments, which have become increasingly available in recent years, offer opportunities to transfer risk to outside parties. Although the finance department is responsible for these tools in many organizations, procurement has a significant role to play.

Risk can be transferred directly through raw-material hedges, physical hedges, and currency options. It can also be transferred indirectly, by way of energy hedges, weather hedges, and synthetic hedges that respond to changes in a secondary underlying variable. Futures and derivative commodity exchanges, such as the Chicago Mercantile Exchange and the London Metal Exchange, now provide wide arrays of futures ranging from dairy to livestock to forestry products. Additionally, several insurance companies offer customized contracts for specific applications and focus on supplier-side risks.

Weather hedging is an interesting component of synthetic hedging. A Hungarian poultry processor has explored weather hedging to mitigate the risks of rising prices for wheat, which it uses as bird feed and which is also a major cost factor. There is a direct correlation between sunshine hours in April and wheat prices. Consequently, betting on a high number of sunshine hours can be used as a synthetic hedge to mitigate the risk of high wheat prices. Insurance companies offer such hedges.

Big nonfinancial players, including Lufthansa, Stora Enso, and AstraZeneca, use advanced trading instruments in highly volatile raw-material markets.[18] Lufthansa has a dedicated team for hedging and trading for fuel using such instruments as calls, puts, swaps, and basic option combinations. Stora Enso's global energy department uses instruments such as physical long-term contracts and financial derivatives (hedging in energy and pulp and paper).

Physical hedging is another opportunity. By managing inventory placement in strategic locations—ideally, the supplier's location—companies are able to react quickly to demand changes both globally and locally. Locations are strategically positioned to allow for fast and inexpensive switching among suppliers in different geographies, as well as to maintain duplicate inventories as protection from location-specific disruptions. Future leaders will maintain optimal inventory levels by balancing

---

[18]Dragana Pilipovic, *Energy Risk: Valuing and Managing Energy Derivatives*, 2nd ed. (New York: McGraw-Hill, 2007).

multiple criteria, including the timing of sales and procurement contracts, the seasonality of raw-material prices, the forecasted demand, and the forecasted supply availability.

Using Design to Switchability

Agile companies have made "design to switchability" the centerpiece of their end-to-end production processes for certain products. Daimler, for example, constantly shifts between rhodium and palladium as the key element in its exhaust cleaning systems. A leading European producer of noncarbonated soft drinks switches between different sweetener types depending on their cost levels.

In the chemical industry, a global company had prepared for potential price volatility by designing products that could easily switch from one sourcing material to a less costly alternative. By having design to switchability in place, the company was able to respond efficiently to spikes in its primary feedstock by shifting to a substitute feedstock that was 25 percent less expensive and also required 10 percent less volume in the manufacturing process. Moreover, the company was able to easily switch between the two feedstocks as circumstances warranted.

Some food companies, for example, have processes that enable liquid, ingot, crystal, and powder sugar types to be interchanged. Another approach is for companies to establish functional specifications that allow them to vary the compositions of different raw materials, for example by changing the types of nuts and raisins used in nut mixtures.

What do these companies have in common? In each case, procurement took the lead in demonstrating how the ability to switch between input factors could improve costs. Procurement category managers at these companies gained the right to form cross-functional teams to develop specifications based on the ability to switch input factors. To seize opportunities, they have set up processes to activate switching based on market conditions.

A variation on modularity is to design recyclability into products or to design them with fewer components. This is the concept underlying "design to cost." A company can reduce its exposure to volatility if it can use fewer materials by, for example, making packaging thinner or using recycled paper for its cardboard. A leading global retailer requested that all of its suppliers reduce the amount of packaging materials by 10 percent within two years. In addition to receiving a favorable response from the public, the company saved significant money by asking the suppliers to share the savings they gained.

Forecasting and Shaping Customer Demand

Influencing and shaping demand to align with supply volatility will be an increasingly important strategy to achieve smoother production and protect margin. The objective is to adjust the demand, volume, and product mix according to price fluctuations and availability of inputs so that companies can sell products more aggressively during their high-margin period.

Pricing and price promotions are the conventional techniques for doing this. Other ways to direct demand to products in excess supply include changing default choices on websites. Strategic product placement, internal sales incentives, staggered shipment agreements, and deferring revenue can also be effective.

A leading soft-drink company heavily promoted the diet version of its product when prices for sugar (an ingredient of its nondiet beverage that only recently began to experience price volatility) skyrocketed by 60 percent. A global chewing-gum company similarly promoted alternatively flavored products when peppermint prices reached extremely high levels.

Many other effective practices have been deployed, but very few players have so far combined all possible levers and focused on the most relevant risks to preemptively mitigate. That makes it critical to determine how to react (ideally, companies will react in a way that allows them not only to weather the downturn but actually to profit) once disruptions and volatility occur, which we discuss next.

Reacting Faster and Smarter Than the Competition

Agility differentiates companies that simply react to disruptions and volatility from those able to profit from it. To illustrate the possibilities, consider the different ways two electronics companies reacted to a supplier disaster when lightning struck a mutual supplier's semiconductor plant, causing a fire that contaminated millions of chips. The supplier lost $40 million in sales, representing less than 0.6 percent of sales volume. Its biggest customers were these two electronics players.

The first one did not actively respond to the disruption and accepted the supplier's estimation that full production would return in a week. By the time the companies discovered, weeks later, that production would be severely compromised, the second player had already claimed the supplier's alternative capacity. The first company reported long-term losses of several billion U.S. dollars, attributable in part to the incident at the supplier's plant. In contrast, the second company reacted aggressively to the disruption. Its flexible supply chain strategy allowed it to switch suppliers quickly and reengineer some products to accept alternative chips. As a result, its production line was relatively unaffected. Profits at that time rose by 42 percent and market share increased from 27 percent to 30 percent in the first six months after the fire.

Having a clear view of the raw-material market allows for informed decisions and better planning with respect to future bottom-line impacts. Procurement leaders will track market fluctuations of supplier prices that affect COGS. This includes tracking current commodity prices and forecasting future prices, and using component analysis to estimate cost pressures for each commodity price scenario relevant to the company and its competitors.

Procurement leaders will also closely monitor their suppliers' environment and, to the extent possible, provide support to facilitate long-term stability and thereby encourage the early detection of risks.

Additionally, companies should develop playbooks to provide a detailed guide to the actions that should be taken across functions and the individuals responsible for them.

In 2008, Fujitsu put in place a disaster-response strategy that enabled all seven of its production plants affected by the 2011 Japanese earthquake and tsunami to resume regular operations at 100 percent production capacity within a month.

Fujitsu operates semiconductor manufacturing facilities in multiple regions so that unaffected regions can pick up the slack if one region is hit by a disaster. In response to the 2011 events, the company temporarily transferred a portion of the production line of desktop PCs from Fujitsu Isotec Ltd. to Fujitsu Shimane Ltd., located in unaffected regions. It also implemented provisions of its flexible supplier contracts to adjust volumes across regions and implemented plans set out in playbooks to restore electricity, water, and other utilities at disaster-stricken plants. Fujitsu was recognized for achieving the most rapid and efficient recovery among all Japanese semiconductor suppliers.

Building Agile Procurement in Three Steps

Agile procurement requires the ability to detect and to respond; the required response must feature cross-functional coordination. These capabilities will not be built by simply improving current methods and processes. To perform its expanded role, procurement needs to significantly upgrade the tools and skill sets in its arsenal. Agile procurement represents a significant step-up in the function's capabilities, and can be built in three steps.

Step 1: Defining the Relevant Uncertainty

In the future, procurement officers will increasingly hear questions like "How exposed are we to raw-material volatility?" and "How healthy are our key suppliers?" While these questions are not new, they are becoming more relevant. To provide answers and be able to reliably predict and calibrate resource conditions, broader categories of risk must be embedded into the procurement strategy.

BROADER PERSPECTIVE Agile procurement enables procurement officers to look further afield, to a whole spectrum of upstream, macroeconomic, and exogenous factors that can jeopardize the supply chain and disrupt global footprints. Procurement must consider how events that trigger volatility are linked, including changes in such factors as raw-material availability and pricing, relationships with suppliers, and the status of the supplier's suppliers. Procurement leaders must recognize that volatility can have an impact not only on materials costs but also on brand, reputation, and competitive positioning.

UNCERTAINTY ANALYSIS The ability to quantify uncertainty at different nodes of the supply chain remains a distant goal. Short of this step-leap in metrics, however, procurement can capture opportunities by applying an improved uncertainty analysis. The path forward will emphasize business intelligence rather than data. By focusing on the risks that really matter, a procurement organization can begin to integrate internal supply chains seamlessly with external ecosystems. The lesson here is clear: When it comes to being able to translate advanced warning signs into a timely response, "less is more."

DEFINING RELEVANT RISK TYPES To determine where the most dangerous exposure exists and thus which critical areas to monitor, agile procurement divides its risk universe into four broad categories of scrutiny:

1. *Market price volatility* includes raw-material prices on all tier levels, currency exchange rates, energy costs, and inflation.
2. *External event-driven uncertainties* include scarcity, natural disasters, political crises, and new governmental regulations.
3. *Supply and upstream uncertainties* include supplier insolvencies as well as compliance, quality, and capacity issues.

4. *Demand and downstream uncertainties* include changing consumer preferences, competition, product liability, and the emergence of new uses for inputs (such as the diversion of food crops into biofuel production).

It is vital to conduct a procurement risk analysis from a holistic perspective. Companies should assess all of the risk types to understand their exposure. For raw-material volatility, companies should identify the following:

- The annual volatility of prices for the top raw materials (weighted index) during the past three years.
- Raw-material costs as a percentage of total COGS.
- The percentage increase in raw-material costs that can be passed downstream.

For labor rates, companies should identify the following:

- The average annual volatility in wage rates in the top three sourcing locations (including their own facilities) during the past three years.
- Labor costs as a percentage of total COGS (including an estimated labor component for suppliers).

This initial understanding of the company's risk universe can be applied in a cross-functional workshop, which can be used to ensure that the full breadth of the company's expertise is applied. Procurement should prioritize supply uncertainties according to their likelihood and their potential impact on key elements of the business (for example, revenues, costs, service levels, brand). By starting with as broad a set of risks as possible (as many as 25 different types) and making initial estimates of their potential impact, companies can usually identify five to 10 key risks upon which to focus.

Step 2: Quantify Exposure to Risk and Prepare Response Options

Once key uncertainties have been prioritized, the next task is to develop a heat map based on the size of exposure and current levels of response readiness. A threshold of acceptable risk is defined; beyond this threshold, the company is prepared to act.

MEASURING EXPOSURE Where exposure is difficult to quantify, such as determining when the risk of supplier quality issues could disrupt the availability of a highly engineered bespoke component, companies can use failure modes and effects analysis (FMEA) to define response plans. In this approach, a carefully defined rating scale is used to quantify the impact, likelihood, and preparedness for each potential uncertainty.

Market risk exposure can be broadly quantified by analyzing historical and likely future price volatility. Examples include crude oil and currency. Within these categories, companies can adopt a quantitative approach in which probability and available responses are modeled using statistical simulation techniques. For example, Monte Carlo simulation can be applied to estimate the outcomes of different contracting strategies in different scenarios. Key characteristics of future scenarios, such as the evolution of iron ore availability for steel, should be identified and statistically modeled. Based on a combination of contract characteristics, different contract models should then be defined. Using a Monte Carlo simulation, the company can determine the expected average purchase price of steel and the related risk for each contract/ scenario combination. There are several alternatives to Monte Carlo simulation, such as the partial least squares (PLS) method and the finite element method (FEM).

Providing the ability to render a risk quotient in comparative metrics is one of the great promises of the agility paradigm. But even where risk exposure is difficult to measure, companies can have mitigating responses at the ready.

NATURAL OWNER OF RISK To decide which risks to own strategically, a firm should sort through all the risks in its portfolio, current and future, and consider two critical variables—the natural risk ownership and the ability to influence the risk.

The company should determine the natural risk ownership based on a thorough assessment that considers three lines of defense (and the competitive advantages that come along with them).

Resilience of the Business Model As we saw in the economic crisis, subtle differences in business models can yield substantial differences in risk exposure. Consider a gas distributor that had significant flexibility in both its supply contracts and its sales agreements. When sales fell as customers retrenched, it was affected only on the margin.

Risk Management and Mitigation Skills This is defined by the ability of a firm to pull the agile procurement levers as described earlier.

Financial Strength and Shareholder Alignment Sufficient capital is the key to financial resilience, and has been the traditional focus of efforts to define the risk appetite. But we argue that companies should regard financial power as their last line of defense. Their understanding of financial strength should take a multiyear perspective, rather than a single-year perspective; should be updated regularly as the environment changes; and should be compared with the financial strengths of rivals. The combination of natural risk ownership and the ability to influence the outcomes of risks that become realities will dictate one of four strategies.

If a firm has clear evidence that it has the natural ownership of the risk but is unable to influence it, the firm should (1) accept the risk as is, along with the upside or downside. However, if the risk is one that can be understood and thus influenced, the firm should (2) develop capabilities to learn about the risk and mitigate it to gain the upside that comes from superior knowledge and information.

If the company is not the natural owner, it should seek to (3) transfer the risk to a customer or supplier or to a third party (for example, through a hedge or insurance). In some cases, this might require paying a premium. If the risk can be influenced, the company should (4) partner with a better owner that can help it obtain an upside through better knowledge.[19]

A company's definition of acceptable risk must be framed in terms of both specific value chains and more holistic corporate business objectives. In addition to financial objectives in terms of revenues, gross profits, and growth rate on sales, these objectives must include longer-term enterprise goals in such areas as product development, competitive positioning, marketing, and branding.

In determining risk appetite in the context of agile procurement, the fundamental question to ask is not "How much risk you can take?" but rather "How much risk do you want to actually bear before triggering preventive action?"

RANGE OF RISK Risks that have only a small financial impact can have a major effect on a company's strategic objectives, making their consequences significant but more difficult to measure. One pharmaceutical company, for example, was the sole manufacturer of a lifesaving medicine that accounted for a relatively small share of revenues and profits; any supply failure, however, would have been catastrophic for patients given that no substitute was available. Such an event would render devastating harm to the company's reputation. A thorough procurement risk inventory will identify exposure in these areas, which traditional analyses have typically neglected. To fully benefit from agile procurement, it is imperative that companies assess and be prepared to respond to factors that, while

---

[19]David Apgar, *Risk Intelligence: Learning to Manage What We Don't Know* (Boston: Harvard Business Press, 2006).

perhaps less immediately damaging to financial results, could ultimately inflict a more lasting injury.

Step 3: Develop and Implement Cross-Functional Agile Procurement Levers

Understanding their current exposure to key risks allows companies to make informed choices about their ability and willingness to respond to them. Such decisions, however, are not straightforward, and responses are not automatically undertaken.

Various criteria and capabilities influence actions. These include a company's risk policies and willingness to expose itself to risk (the afore-mentioned risk appetite), the availability and cost of mitigating actions, and the nature of the upside opportunities enabled by those actions. A company must apply different agile procurement levers to mitigate the different risks that arise based on its approach to these considerations.

Procurement will not be able to handle this alone. It must build a senior, cross-functional team to determine the enterprise's priorities, while being clear on the role procurement should play to best support the team.

This cross-functional team approach to procurement allows for a fuller understanding of risk and a shared understanding of total cost across the value chain. This is in stark contrast to the more limited perspective when uncertainties are viewed in terms of individual projects. The participation of marketing in the decision-making process, for example, enables rapid feedback on the marketing mix and rates as well as visibility of expansion plans into new products and markets. By working with engineering, procurement can help ensure robust product design that uses industry-standard components whenever possible and has the ability to change materials and specifications rapidly when confronted with risk. Finance's knowledge of currency fluctuations and raw-material costs should also be applied in the decision-making process. Suppliers can be included on the team to offer input from their external viewpoints.

Failure to integrate cross-functionally can lead to a costly misalignment of efforts. A classic example is what happens when procurement is uninformed by sales about customer contracts that prohibit the company from passing along increases in material costs. In such circumstances, if procurement agrees during a volatile period to pay a higher price for material to ensure availability, but sales is locked into nonnegotiable contracts, the company is forced to assume the full cost of mitigating supply risk. If procurement had participated in cross-functional risk management, however, other agile procurement levers might have been at its disposal to cope with the volatility and reduce the impact on the company.

PREEMPTIVE AGILE PROCUREMENT LEVERS Preemptive agile procurement levers are put in place before a disruptive event occurs. These tend to be preparatory initiatives, intended to reduce the likely impact of uncertainty on the organization or to improve its future ability to respond.

As discussed earlier, these levers include strategic decisions about whether to make or buy, backward integration or direct sourcing options, supplier footprint decisions, and single or multiple sourcing. They also include choices about the level and location of inventory, such as the use of safety stocks or speculative stocks to capture the benefits of temporary drops in raw-material prices.

DETECTIVE AGILE PROCUREMENT LEVERS Detective agile procurement levers are techniques companies use to get advance warning about pending volatility and scarcities faster, giving them more time to preempt or respond to uncertainties.

Effective detection requires companies to monitor a broad range of indicators, among them overall market evolution in terms of customers' and competitors' performance, new product introduction, and regulation. Key indicators of potential supply distress, such as changes to quality, cost, or delivery performance, must be monitored. Political, economic, and environmental changes at suppliers' locations are increasingly important in a volatile environment.

On the external side, relevant material includes analyst and broker reports, journals, press releases, and competitor information. Such internal measures as stock levels, order backlogs, and market expectations are consulted. Information technology (IT) infrastructure and analytical capabilities enable insights and predictions to be rapidly drawn from these data.

RESPONSIVE AGILE PROCUREMENT LEVERS Responsive agile procurement entails actions that companies plan but do not execute until certain predefined conditions occur. It requires the design of clearly understood contingency plans (critical information requirements, if/then protocols, and triggers) and the coordination of those plans with involved suppliers. It defines the setup of teams with clear decision rights, capabilities, and connections to all relevant actors.

Finally, after every event that triggers a response, it is imperative to incorporate the lessons from the experience into the procurement process to raise it to higher levels of agile procurement. Leaders employ top-to-top meetings to leverage these lessons in procurement discussions with the top management teams of key suppliers and customers, collaborating with them in after-action reviews. They also activate senior cross-functional leadership teams to identify new strategic sourcing opportunities.

How Hewlett-Packard Manages Component Cost Uncertainties

Hewlett-Packard (HP) has managed component cost uncertainties through a rigorous supplier risk management program using probabilities to build scenarios and calculate the variability of parts and manufactured commodities. These programs are managed through cross-functional processes with procurement, finance, sales and marketing, and supply chain all working in vertical alignment.[20]

Procurement contracts reflect different approaches to risk sharing with suppliers to maximize the assurance and the stability of supply. HP takes ownership of risks it can bear more cheaply; suppliers take on those risks that they can better manage. For products with low demand uncertainty, HP commits to specific quantities in return for price discounts. Products with high demand uncertainty are procured through open-market or spot-market transactions.

This has resulted in a higher level of agile procurement as well as substantial cost savings. Improvement has been achieved in the assurance and stability of the supply of several commodities for which the company had previously experienced shortages. Costs have become more predictable, as the company manages cost uncertainty and protects margins by including specific pricing terms in contracts. Inventory has been reduced internally and at supplier locations by several percentage points thanks to greater agility in product introductions. The company has also achieved incremental material cost discounts of greater than 5 percent through quantity commitments that lower supplier demand risks and enable more efficient supplier planning and production.

The company has realized U.S. $445 million in cost savings over the past six years out of a cumulative spend of $23 billion. Of that savings, $345 million came from material costs savings, $50 million was related to profit protected from commodity shortages, and $50 million stemmed from cost predictability.

---

[20]Venu Nagali, Jerry Hwang, David Sanghera, Matt Gaskins, Mark Pridgen, Tim Thurston, Patty Mackenroth, Dwight Branvold, Patrick Scholler, and Greg Shoemaker, "Procurement Risk Management (PRM) at Hewlett-Packard Company," *Interfaces* 38, no. 1 (January/February 2008): 51–60.

Making Agile Procurement Stick

To become and remain an agile organization in the emerging business environment of continual volatility, companies must apply several key enablers.

Distinctive Cross-Functional Integration across the Enterprise

Procurement's mission is to seamlessly integrate the internal procurement organization with an internal and external ecosystem, including suppliers and suppliers' suppliers. Cross-functional category teams, which previously would be organized largely on a project basis, should become an integral part of the organizational landscape. These teams possess a shared understanding of total cost across the value chain (including, for example, stock-out costs and inbound and outbound freight).

An advanced procurement organization has rapid feedback loops on product mix and rates from marketing and is involved in the planning of expansion into new segments and markets. It works with engineering to ensure robust product designs that use industry-standard components whenever possible, and has the ability to change materials and specifications quickly. It is tightly linked with finance and treasury on raw materials and currencies. Suppliers participate in select product development decision-making processes. In addition, procurement is at the table when decisions are being reached about make versus buy, backward integration, and manufacturing footprint.

Dedicated Personnel with Robust Skill Sets

Procurement has a central role in agile procurement, but to obtain ownership it must possess the required skill set. Procurement needs to have dedicated supplier development, intelligence, and process enablement staff in place. For many companies, this might require an investment in new skill sets, but these skills will be crucial for the future. Category managers must be trained on advanced supply-chain agile procurement tools such as cash flow at risk (CFaR) analysis across the entire value chain, total cost of ownership (TCO) model development, linear programming/network optimization, and supply chain scenario modeling. Key members of the procurement team must have a deep understanding of the value chain, including supply and demand balance and trends, a technical understanding of product functionality, and the ability to anticipate technology disruptions.

Agile Infrastructure

Procurement needs to develop a toolbox, practices, and forums that support agile procurement beyond risk management. This tactical repertoire includes contract clauses that allow flexibility (such as a TCO-based meet-or-release clause that will make it possible for the company to switch to other suppliers, clear key performance indicators [KPIs] and performance targets that allow for contract termination if not met, and a robust force majeure clause); automated tools and templates for analysis and visibility into the supply chain (such as a tool for spend analysis, cost pressure models, dashboards for main commodities and risks, as well as driver charts interpreting demand and supply factors to determine future commodity prices); and a rapid certification process for suppliers and supplier quality.

Rapid Decision Making and Processes

The capacity to trigger decisions quickly is critical for the effective management of risk and disruptions. To gain the required speed, it is imperative to have in place preapproved strategies based on possible scenarios that can be quickly implemented (deplete inventory when prices go down, for example, and build it when prices go up), clear tracking, and definition of triggers that launch specific responses. Governance mechanisms must clearly indicate who decides what, and what information needs to be reviewed prior to action. A rapid deployment committee should have sufficiently senior personnel to command respect.

■ ■ ■

Four aspirations should guide entrepreneurial CPOs as they seek to lead their procurement organizations to achieve these objectives in the new era of volatility. Procurement must seek to become:

- Deeply networked and embedded into the dynamic global and local sourcing markets in order to develop foresight.
- An agile, decisive actor that quickly spots business issues and seizes the opportunities arising from environmental changes to create competitive advantages.
- The gatekeeper and chief risk officer for the company's access to resources, leveraging sophisticated tools for both financial and physical risk management to secure resources.
- Organized to respond to the changing world by adapting buying behavior, rhythm, contracts, and hedging strategies.

Several risks that agile procurement seeks to address entail the management of environmental, social, and regulatory (ESR) issues. Dealing with these issues from the perspective not only of risk management but also of opportunity creation will become a priority for CPOs in the future. The next chapter looks at why these issues have become so prominent and how CPOs can deal with ESR issues to contain associated costs and risks as well as to create new opportunities.

The New Economic Drivers: Capturing the Total Impact of Environmental, Social, and Regulatory Factors

Main Messages

- Environmental, social, and regulatory (ESR) issues will become increasingly important, presenting procurement with new costs, risks, and opportunities.
- Governments and consumers will make educated and significant decisions on ESR; as a result, functions, including procurement, will have to anticipate and prepare.
- To incorporate ESR into sourcing decisions sustainably, procurement must define a comprehensive approach based on total impact of ownership (TIO) considerations.

Consider this scenario: An environmental organization accuses your company of sourcing ingredients from a supplier whose practices result in the destruction of rain forests and orangutan habitats. To raise public awareness, the organization sends more than 200,000 e-mails and launches a social media campaign—the centerpiece of which is a YouTube video that shows a consumer opening one of your company's products and discovering a bloody orangutan finger.

Does this seem improbable? It shouldn't. Greenpeace launched just such a campaign against Nestlé in 2010 in an effort to change the practices of one of the company's palm-oil suppliers in Indonesia. To address the brand damage in the short term, Nestlé suspended all sourcing from the supplier and partnered with The Forest Trust (TFT) to analyze its palm-oil supply chain. Over the longer term, the company has applied a new lens to its supply chain to account for its environmental and social impacts, recognizing that value for shareholders is tied to creating value for the communities in which it operates.

Or consider this: Your company has decided to dispose of a major physical asset that poses environmental risks. The disposal approach selected is well aligned with what several scientists regard as the best available alternative, and even the publication *Nature* applauds your plans. Nevertheless, activists seize your asset and stage a savvy protest campaign in the media; as a result, customers boycott your product. After weeks of insisting on the scientific validity of your plans, you finally give in and dispose of the asset using an alternative approach that carries far more risks for the environment and results in significant criticism from the scientific community. Do you think this can't happen? It can. It happened to Shell when that company wanted to dispose of the Brent Spar oil platform by sinking it to the ocean floor. Scientists agreed that the polluted platform did not pose a threat to deepwater organisms, although it would be very dangerous to organisms in shallow water. Even so, Greenpeace activists staged a protest, and public opinion forced Shell to tow the platform to shore, which brought with it substantial risk of polluting the shallow waters.[1]

As these examples demonstrate, new economic drivers beyond classical supply-price considerations are having an increasing impact on sourcing decisions. Environmental, social, and regulatory (ESR) considerations are poised to become key decision-making variables for CPOs as they select suppliers of goods and services. Their increasing importance is driven by many factors and has been accelerated by the technological revolution we discussed in Chapter 5, "Big Data and the Global Grid: Procurement's New Role in Data-Driven Decision Making." Companies must proactively change their approach to procurement to avoid negative outcomes, such as increased costs and heightened risks, even as they seek to capture value-generating opportunities.

ESR issues are taking center stage and will continue to raise costs and risks as well as create new opportunities for procurement. Consequently, CPOs will need to think about the possibilities for coping with the challenges and capturing the opportunities.

---

[1]"Brent Spar Dossier," Shell, May 2008, accessed March 7, 2013, http://s02.static-shell.com/content/dam/shell-new/local/country/gbr/downloads/e-and-p/brent-spar-dossier.pdf.

ESR Issues Take Center Stage in Procurement

When the aforementioned campaign happened, Nestlé had already been working for several years on an advanced set of ESR policies. The Greenpeace campaign, among other drivers, led Nestlé to become a global leader in ESR issues. Nestlé launched a comprehensive program aimed at protecting the environment and helping the communities in which it operates to prosper. To accomplish this mission, the company is not just changing the way it operates but looking to transform its entire supply chain and supplier ecosystem.

Nestlé has established supplier partnerships and developed extensive programs in cocoa and coffee production to develop farmers' capabilities. It provides training as well as higher-yielding plants, enabling farmers to run profitable farms and eliminate child labor while ensuring a sustainable supply chain for the company. Nestlé has also launched extensive environmental programs, which include supporting business partners in developing management systems and helping farmers improve irrigation and water-management practices.

Nestlé has developed a systematic set of tools and approaches to assess and improve the impact of sourcing decisions on the environment. For bottled water, as an example, it uses standardized tools to evaluate the impact of its packaging as well as its environmental footprint. In applying such tools, it is partnering with recognized life-cycle assessment scientists and experts.[2]

In addition, the company is developing a multicriteria ecodesign tool called Eco-D that covers both packaging and ingredients in all product categories. Eco-D takes into account the entire life cycle of the company's products, using environmental indicators such as climate change, land use, ecosystem quality, mineral and nonrenewable resources, and water consumption.[3]

Nestlé has also created a "vendor approval compass," with an explicit focus on responsible sourcing. It has a Responsible Sourcing Audit program to assess supplier compliance with the Nestlé Supplier Code. During 2010 and 2011, Nestlé food safety and quality auditors reassessed and approved each of the company's high-risk vendors. The company has also launched an extensive traceability program, intended to map key supply chain inputs to their origin.

---

[2] "Life Cycle Approach," Nestlé, accessed February 25, 2013, www.nestle.com/csv/environment/lifecycleapproach.

[3] "Applying Eco-Design," Nestlé, accessed February 25, 2013, www.nestle.com/csv/Environment/lifecycleapproach/Applyingeco-design.

Organizations are not undertaking ESR initiatives exclusively for brand or image management. Many companies see a significant cost advantage in marrying sustainability with their sourcing decisions.

Take Nespresso, which launched an initiative to build its capacity to collect used capsules for recycling and to source aluminum responsibly. The company has put in place collection systems that will triple its capacity and allow for the recycling of 75 percent of used capsules by 2013. In addition to the significant material cost savings, remelting the aluminum requires only 5 percent of the energy needed for its primary production. In addition, Nespresso is working with the International Union for Conservation of Nature (IUCN) and major aluminum producers to promote a standard for more sustainable aluminum sourcing.

Similarly, Wal-Mart, as part of its Sustainability 360 plan, is working with its suppliers globally to reduce packaging by 5 percent in its supply chain by 2013, equivalent to preventing 660,000 tons of carbon dioxide from entering the atmosphere. In one initiative, Wal-Mart developed a packaging scorecard to help evaluate the sustainability of its suppliers' packaging.[4] The company's buyers use the scorecard to make more informed procurement decisions. As an additional benefit, Wal-Mart is also achieving cost savings through reduced packaging costs.

These companies are not alone. For almost all companies, ESR issues are becoming increasingly important in procurement decisions. Three driving forces stand out: public awareness, increasing factor costs, and government activism.

Public Awareness

Consumers and communities are becoming increasingly conscious of the environment and corporate social responsibility, an awareness that is amplified by easy access to information via connectivity enabled by the global grid, discussed in Chapter 5. In an age of instant connectivity, previously local issues can go viral and have a major global impact on a company's brand image and revenues. Greenpeace's campaign against Nestlé demonstrated a trend: special-interest groups are harnessing the power of social media and the Internet to target networks of engaged consumers to promote their agendas. As the number of social media users continues to expand globally, the audience for such campaigns increases—along with the risks to businesses. What is unclear, however, is the extent to which ESR issues will influence consumers to change their commercial behavior.

---

[4]"Wal-Mart Unveils 'Packaging Scorecard' to Suppliers," Wal-Mart, accessed February 22, 2013, http://news.walmart.com/news-archive/2006/11/01/wal-mart -unveils-packaging-scorecard-to-suppliers.

Increasing Factor Costs

Energy prices have increased significantly in recent years, and, as discussed in Chapter 6, "Volatility as the New Normal: Translating Sourcing Risk into Competitive Advantage," prices for the raw materials used for packaging, such as polyethylene, glass, and paper, are extremely volatile. In addition, prices have increased for waste and waste removal. Companies have recognized that they can reduce costs as well as improve their green image by focusing on efficiencies in these areas.

Government Activism

Governments are setting stricter regulations, which have the potential to disrupt entire supply chains. Consider, for example, how requirements to reduce carbon emissions would affect agriculture. Efforts to minimize emissions, such as no-till planting, would be felt throughout the supply chain, including by equipment manufacturers, seed suppliers, and fertilizer providers.

Governments are not only setting stricter regulations, but also becoming more active, which has resulted in the need to strategically manage a more dynamic regulatory landscape. In an increasingly connected world, governments are taking active measures to attract capital investment, protect local industries, and manage economic volatility. This often takes the form of interventions such as subsidies, customs duties, and local content requirements in sourcing. China is a case in point. To promote exports, the Chinese government provides massive subsidies to industries such as solar-panel manufacturing while at the same time limiting access to rare earth supplies, as described in Chapter 3, "The Great Global Rebalancing: Building a Dynamic Sourcing Footprint."

There are other examples of government initiatives. Many countries impose import tariffs that limit the trade of dairy goods, for instance.

Tax breaks are another commonly applied form of government intervention. Singapore's attractive tax regime has made that country a magnet for companies seeking to set up sourcing hubs in Asia. The same is true for Switzerland and some other countries in Europe.

New Costs, Risks, and Opportunities

The increasing importance of ESR issues has given rise to new costs and risks related to procurement and supply management, which companies must consider when making sourcing decisions. Increasingly, ESR issues have also created new opportunities for those forward-looking companies that sought them out.

New Costs

ESR issues have several implications relating to procurement costs. These effects might be the direct costs of environmental input factors such as energy, water, air, or ground or indirect costs in the form of taxes or transactional costs on current input factors. Operational costs relating to energy, water, and waste management may increase, although implementing efficiency measures may reduce costs over the longer term. Moreover, governments are imposing additional taxes, duties, and tariffs, such as import tariffs and CO_2 taxes.

Companies will also incur higher procurement costs as they change practices to comply with increasingly numerous and burdensome regulatory requirements (such as emissions permits, performance standards, and local sourcing quotas) as well as new industry norms (for example, if the Forest Stewardship Council [FSC] standard for wood becomes more commonly applied, consumer expectations will increase). Imagine a European Union carbon emissions tax: If you assume certification costs for your carbon emissions management system to be on the order of the cost for ISO 9001/14001 certification, depending on size, you will pay between €100,000 and several million euros for the certification. Multiply this by approximately 500,000 relevant companies in Europe, and the costs for the system would easily reach billions of euros.

In this context, costs to ensure supplier compliance would increase, such as the costs incurred to measure and audit suppliers' ESR performance and systems. However, if suppliers struggle to keep up with new ESR standards, those suppliers that succeed in meeting the standards will be able to command higher prices.

Heightened Risks

ESR issues also create critical risks that must be considered in sourcing decisions. Cost implications, stricter regulations, and increased environmental awareness have increased the likelihood that companies will incur both direct cleanup costs and potential brand damage from incidents that harm the environment or endanger community health. Brand damage is a particularly critical risk, and one that could arise from practices throughout the supply chain—including the practices of upstream suppliers. Companies that fail to address ESR issues throughout the supply chain also risk losing their social license to operate. This risk makes it critical to manage the ESR performance of both direct and upstream suppliers and to maintain strong relationships with regulatory bodies and local communities. From a legal perspective, companies could face the risk of penalties for noncompliance, and they may even find themselves accused of complicity in a supplier's misconduct.

New Opportunities

Just as total quality management demonstrated that the pursuit of higher quality does not necessarily result in higher costs, superior ESR performance need not negatively impact the bottom line. But companies must capture the new opportunities ESR creates. These include the following.

REDUCED TOTAL COSTS As described previously, some companies have discovered that integrating good ESR practices into procurement decisions may actually lead to lower costs and greater value in the long term. By developing suppliers and setting standards, companies can improve productivity and reduce costs in the supply chain. For example, beverage companies have reduced the weight and corresponding costs of their bottled-water containers by drastically altering the design to reduce the amount of plastic used. In the past, consumers would have considered these bottles to be of low quality; however, branding the bottles as environmentally conscious has enabled the companies to gain consumer acceptance. This new "ESR design to cost (DTC)" is characterized by turning the design of goods and services into solutions. Although consumers readily identify these design changes as reductions in quality, they also positively associate the new designs with environmental or social benefits.

NEW MARKETS AND PRODUCTS New markets are arising in response to new regulations and standards as well as in response to consumer demand. Examples of such markets include European and Australian emissions-trading systems (although these systems have not met initial ramp-up expectations), energy-efficient solutions, and carbon-footprint auditing. Also, by improving their brand image, companies have the opportunity to capture and retain those consumers who place a premium on ESR performance. New products that have entered markets in recent years in response to ESR-related demand include fair-trade coffee and energy-efficient materials used in the construction industry.

BETTER QUALITY AND CONSISTENCY By implementing ESR supplier-management systems and development programs, companies can improve quality and consistency throughout the supply chain. In the course of our work with many clients, we have observed that suppliers that demonstrate a commitment to ESR tend also to provide higher quality and greater consistency than their peers. For example, a global electronics company has found a direct correlation between the ESR standards and quality standards of its supplier base. In many instances, this improvement simply reflects transparency in the supply chain; with transparency comes resolution of ESR issues.

IMPROVING INDUSTRY STRUCTURE Increasing the focus on ESR issues in an industry can raise the bar for industry standards, which helps ensure that new entrants adhere to the same standards as incumbents, thereby maintaining barriers to entry. Companies can also work with government and regulatory bodies to create a favorable structure for a supply industry.

MOTIVATING EMPLOYEES Companies in all industries can create value by attracting and retaining talent. Members of the workforce, in keeping with the public at large, are becoming more aware of ESR issues. Companies must ensure that they are not losing high-quality talent as a consequence of dissatisfaction with ESR performance. For example, a leading global packaged-goods company requires that ESR actions are included in each employee's objectives, and employees must understand their role in achieving the ESR goals. While this engages the employees internally, thus creating more awareness and pride, it also creates a set of brand ambassadors who increasingly express themselves across all kinds of social media.

Industries are incorporating ESR issues into their business and procurement strategies, but not all are moving at the same pace. Consumer-facing industries, such as consumer goods, and industries that have a high impact on the local community, such as resources industries, are at the forefront because they are under the most pressure from end consumers, communities, governments, and activists. Although these companies initially reacted in response to negative incidents and/or stakeholder pressure, many are now proactively pursuing ESR-related opportunities. Regardless of the catalyst for a company's decision to focus on ESR issues, most companies are evolving toward a greater emphasis on ESR issues in business and procurement strategy.

How Can Procurement Cope?

Clearly, ESR considerations pose significant costs and risks for procurement—but they also present significant opportunities. Leading procurement organizations have developed innovative solutions to address the challenges and capture the opportunities. Many have set the ultimate goal of full traceability. This entails identifying and addressing ESR issues in all aspects of a company's processes, products, and services; doing so requires visibility into the activities of partners across the entire supply chain (not limited to tier 1). Achieving such an ambitious goal will not be easy, and many different routes to this end point may yet take shape. Embedding ESR considerations in procurement strategy is the starting point; as that strategy is put in place, companies should note that systematically managing these issues in the supply chain and building relationships are key enablers.

We illustrate the possibilities by considering how some procurement organizations have already assumed leadership in ESR.

Make ESR a Mandatory Consideration in Defining Procurement Strategy

ESR considerations must be key pillars in the development of procurement and corporate strategies. These issues are already influencing strategy at many companies in different ways. Consider the following examples.

GAINING ACCESS TO NEW MARKETS As we have discussed, new markets can arise when ESR issues are addressed. For example, Siemens recognized that its suppliers had to improve their energy efficiency and that this need created an opportunity to provide services that would turn suppliers into customers. The company created the Energy Efficiency Program for Suppliers (EEP4S), which offers specialized analysis and consulting with regard to suppliers' energy and carbon performance.[5] Functional business units drive this initiative from a content perspective, but the transformation of suppliers into customers results from applying an ESR lens to procurement. As another example, the company ITC has invested heavily in a rural supply chain through its "e-Choupal" initiative.[6] In return, the company has received privileged access to supply and has opened up new markets for its products.

SECURING A LICENSE TO OPERATE This approach is particularly important in the resources industry. Companies must manage their relationships in locations where resources are available to ensure that the local community and governmental authorities support their continued presence. By proactively engaging with the community on environmental and social issues and with the relevant authorities on regulatory issues, companies can prevent ESR issues from arising, build trust among community members, and help to shape regulations. For example, Rio Tinto invests heavily in indigenous employment in Australia and also supports indigenous suppliers and contractors through supplier partnerships and training programs.

SECURING SUPPLY IN A TIGHT MARKET For many companies, commodities are critical inputs. As examples: palm oil and paper are critical for Unilever; coffee and cocoa are essential for Nestlé. Access to supplies will confer a competitive advantage as demand for resources increases and supply is constrained by natural limitations and environmental degradation. By

---

[5]"Efficient Use of Resources," Siemens, accessed February 22, 2013, www .siemens.com/sustainability/en/core-topics/suppliers/management-approach/ resource-efficiency.htm.

[6]"Embedding Sustainability in Business," ITC, accessed February 22, 2013, www .itcportal.com/sustainability/lets-put-india-first/echoupal.aspx.

building partnerships with suppliers, companies can ensure loyalty while they improve the lives of the farmers who supply these commodities. As one example, Unilever has an engagement program for small farms; the program has the dual objectives of increasing farmers' skills, productivity, and income and securing the supply of sustainable crops.[7] The company seeks to incorporate at least 500,000 small farms and 75,000 small-scale distributors in its supply network by 2020.

ELEVATING INDUSTRY NORMS Incumbents can elevate industry norms, thereby raising the barriers to entry for new companies. This places a burden on new entrants to apply the same high standards as current players rather than taking a more lax approach to ESR issues. Wal-Mart, for example, is working with The Sustainability Consortium (TSC) to establish a common language for evaluating product and supplier sustainability performance.[8] The resulting standards would set a higher bar for ESR throughout the retail industry. Likewise, Unilever has established the Sustainable Sourcing Advisory Board (SSAB), which includes external experts, academics, and representatives from nongovernmental organizations (NGOs).[9]

Manage ESR Issues in the Supply Chain More Systematically and Analytically

To implement strategic considerations such as the aforementioned topics, leading companies are moving beyond making decisions based on gut feelings regarding ESR issues to making rigorous business decisions enabled by quantification, comparison, and an understanding of explicit trade-offs. As discussed in Chapter 5, "Big Data and the Global Grid: Procurement's New Role in Data-Driven Decision Making," big data, including highly detailed information, and advanced analytics will provide previously unavailable fact bases and tools for effective decision making. Some possibilities for enabling excellence are the following.

BUILDING A FACT BASE ON ESR ISSUES A detailed fact base will be critical to understanding ESR issues at the local level. For example, compliance with local sourcing regulations is critical in Brazil, whereas some locations in Eastern Europe present major risks with respect to supplier practices.

---

[7]"Unilever Sustainable Living Plan Progress Report 2011," Unilever, accessed February 22, 2013, www.unilever.com/images/uslp-Unilever_Sustainable_Living_Plan_Progress_Report_2011_tcm13-284779.pdf.

[8]"Sustainability Index," Wal-Mart, accessed February 22, 2013, http://corporate.walmart.com/global-responsibility/environment-sustainability/sustainability-index.

[9]"Agricultural Sourcing Partnerships," Unilever, accessed February 25, 2013, www.unilever.com/sustainable-living/sustainablesourcing/agriculturalsourcingpartnerships/index.aspx.

On the positive side, some countries (such as Singapore and Switzerland) offer tax benefits that make them attractive locations for global sourcing functions. Companies must also understand the key ESR risks associated with major sourcing decisions.

APPLYING A TOTAL IMPACT OF OWNERSHIP APPROACH Companies are increasingly using analytical tools and approaches to understand trade-offs in procurement decisions based on quantitative inputs. The traditional total cost of ownership (TCO) approach will be expanded to "total impact of ownership" (TIO)—explicitly capturing the costs, risks, and opportunities arising from ESR issues (see Exhibit 7.1). For example, an aluminum manufacturer that uses coal tar pitch for its smelting operations could buy either liquid or solid pitch. Although a traditional TCO analysis would indicate that solid pitch is the right choice on the basis of cost, a TIO analysis that incorporates health, safety, and environmental risks would indicate that liquid pitch is the better option on the basis of overall impact.

Life-cycle analyses can be used to map the full ESR impact of a product and identify hot spots for action. For example, conducting a life-cycle analysis of a citrus juice product enabled a packaged-goods company to

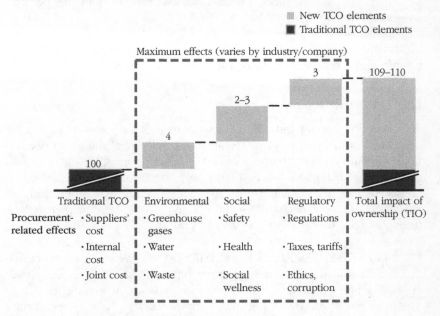

Expected average cost impacts of different ESR influences, percent

EXHIBIT 7.1 New Definition of Total Impact of Ownership (TIO) to Incorporate Environmental, Social, and Regulatory Effects into Sourcing Decisions

Source: McKinsey global survey results, "The Business of Sustainability."

determine that 40 percent of the product's carbon impact resulted from farming, and that the company could substantially reduce this impact by using a low-carbon fertilizer.

SYSTEMATIC ASSESSMENT OF ESR ISSUES Leading companies classify ESR issues into two categories: Nondiscretionary issues are those for which there are no exceptions with respect to compliance. These include child labor laws, ethical issues, and regulatory requirements. For such issues, companies must establish governance and strict compliance criteria. Discretionary issues are those for which decisions need to be made on a case-by-case basis, such as the acceptable level of CO_2 emissions or the use of specific suppliers. These issues are assessed through either a quantitative decision matrix or a subjective, fact-based analysis. For example, a leading global shoe manufacturer uses a sourcing-decision matrix that gives a specific weight to each of several ESR considerations.

MEASUREMENT OF ESR INITIATIVES' IMPACT Companies are starting to use various tools to measure success—not necessarily systematic, full-cost analyses, but specific environmental and social metrics. These include emissions levels, the number of suppliers that the audit process reveals to have improved performance, the volume of packaging saved, the percentage of content made from sustainable sources, and the percentage of locally sourced content. Companies can also use external sources to measure success, including external indexes (such as the Dow Jones Sustainability Index and the Carbon Disclosure Project), sustainability awards, and favorable or unfavorable references in social media.

Build External Relationships

To succeed in coping with ESR issues, companies must look beyond their own borders to build external relationships. Influential industry organizations will emerge as the partners of choice for developing broadly accepted tools and balancing industry and regulatory concerns. The progressive and consistent industry standards they set will become increasingly influential in procurement decisions in the coming decade. Strong partnerships throughout the supply chain will also be critical.

ENGAGING WITH STAKEHOLDERS TO SET INDUSTRY STANDARDS Leading companies are already actively forming partnerships with key external stakeholders and shaping industry debates on sustainability. According to a 2012 McKinsey global survey, 71 percent of companies that are effective in their sustainability agendas form partnerships and engage in active dialogue with key external stakeholders, but only 34 percent of less effective (or ineffective) companies do so. Furthermore, 73 percent of effective companies actively shape public or industry debates on sustainability, while only 25 percent of ineffective companies pursue such activities.[10]

Among the key stakeholders are independent third parties that can set industry-wide standards and provide certification of compliance. Companies can then seek to meet these established standards without having to develop unique programs. For example, the Publishers' Database for Responsible Environmental Paper Sourcing (PREPS database) ranks suppliers based on their compliance with industry standards for pulp and paper.[11] The database was initiated by Pearson and is maintained by an independent consulting company. These industry standards can be used to create a more level playing field. Others have partnered with the Sustainable Apparel Coalition to help create an industry-wide index to measure and evaluate product sustainability. Third parties can also provide superior knowledge of best practices. For example, Coca-Cola partnered with the WWF to identify a significant opportunity to reduce water usage by improving the irrigation practices of its sugar growers.[12]

FOCUSING ON THE FULL SUPPLY CHAIN To embed ESR considerations throughout the entire supply chain, companies should build partnerships with suppliers beyond the first tier. This also involves linking procurement policies with community investment initiatives to ensure a social license to operate. The supplier development process will be critical to achieving this, because many companies are finding that codes and audits are not sufficient to drive value and ensure secure, sustainable partnerships with suppliers. For example, through its Cocoa Plan, Nestlé provides training and higher-yielding plants to cocoa farmers. The goal is to enable farmers to run profitable farms and eliminate child labor, while ensuring a sustainable supply chain for the company. In 2011, the Cocoa Plan resulted in a 55 percent increase in production volumes in Côte d'Ivoire, allowing farmers to earn more than U.S. $500,000 in premiums and bonuses.[13]

[10]"Capturing Value from Sustainability," *McKinseyQuarterly.com*, 2012.

[11]"Process," PREPS, accessed February 25, 2013, http://prepsgroup.com/how.php.

[12]Steven Prokesch, "The Sustainable Supply Chain," *Harvard Business Review*, October 2010.

[13]"Training Farmers," Nestlé, accessed February 25, 2013, www.nestle.com/csv/ruraldevelopment/cocoa/trainingfarmers.

Pursue Full Traceability and Develop Closer Relationships Throughout the Entire Supply Chain

With the appropriate strategic and tactical initiatives in place, companies will be positioned to achieve the goal of full traceability. This goal has already been widely pursued in the food and beverage industry (where it is known as "farm to fork") and in the pharmaceutical industry. We expect this trend to become more evident in other industries as well. For example, the increased awareness regarding "conflict minerals" (that is, those mined in conditions of armed conflict and human rights abuses, such as in the Democratic Republic of the Congo) has become a major concern for high-tech companies. These companies are increasingly looking for ways to improve traceability in their supply chains so that they can avoid sourcing conflict minerals indirectly.

To enhance traceability, some companies are moving beyond basic collaborations by working hand in hand with suppliers to improve outcomes, as well as applying technology to further their efforts and publicize their successes. Companies that provide basic goods and services, such as food, drink, and transportation, may find this fairly easy to accomplish because they have relatively shallow supply chains. However, highly integrated companies that provide complex technical goods or services, like electronic products, cars, and white goods, may find this effort very complex and costly.

CLOSE COLLABORATION TO IMPROVE OUTCOMES Leading companies are already investing in long-term partnerships with suppliers by providing resources and support to help improve outcomes. Setting minimum standards for their suppliers with respect to ESR issues has been critical to this effort. For example, IBM requires tier 1 suppliers to establish and sustain a management system to address their corporate and environmental responsibilities. Suppliers must measure performance and establish quantifiable environmental goals. They also must publicly disclose results associated with these goals and other environmental aspects of the management system.[14]

Similarly, Unilever has partnered with its peers to establish a global task force for responsible sourcing. This task force within the European Brand Association, called AIM-PROGRESS, currently has more than 25 members, including Unilever, Coca-Cola, Nestlé, Danone, Diageo, PepsiCo, Kraft, Colgate-Palmolive, and Procter & Gamble. Its main mission is to develop common methods for evaluating the social and environmental

---

[14]"Supply Chain," IBM, accessed February 25, 2010, www.ibm.com/ibm/environment/supply/.

performance of suppliers across specific groups of goods and services. The goal is to enable the mutual recognition of the audit standards deployed by AIM-PROGRESS members, allowing suppliers to confidently share their audit reports based on an "audit for one is an audit for all" principle.[15] The task force is also engaging in outreach activities with suppliers to raise awareness of responsible sourcing practices and their importance. As a result of the outreach, suppliers are adopting similar practices and adhering to consistent standards.

LEVERAGING TECHNOLOGY The Internet and social media are double-edged swords in this regard. On the one hand, activists can instantly publicize to the entire world any negative ESR issues in a company's supply chain. On the other hand, companies can also use these technologies in their efforts to improve traceability and enhance their brand image. For example, Patagonia, a major apparel company, has a brand image strongly linked to its emphasis on ESR issues. Among its many ESR initiatives, the company insists on full traceability in its supply chain. It has developed an interactive online tool through which it maps its supply chain and provides information to the public about all of its suppliers. The company also requires its suppliers to conduct a similar mapping of their own supply chains. The company has stated that it intends to "use transparency about our supply chain to help us reduce our adverse social and environmental impacts—and on an industrial scale."[16]

New Roles and Capabilities for Procurement

The procurement function is uniquely positioned to spearhead the transformational change required to design and implement the ever-increasing ESR interventions in the supply chain. It has a clear view of the external supply market and the changes in the ESR landscape, as well as a deep understanding of the internal business vision and strategies. For many companies, the effects of ESR are most prevalent in their supply chains, not within their own operations. The majority of energy, emissions, and waste is used or created in their suppliers' value chains, making

---

[15]"Responsible and Sustainable Sourcing: A Guide for our Supply Chain Partners," Unilever, accessed February 26, 2013, www.unilever.com/images/Responsible_and_Sustainable_Sourcing-Standards_guide_for_our_supply_chain_partners%282011%29_tcm13-277604.pdf.

[16]"The Footprint Chronicles," Patagonia, accessed February 26, 2013, www.patagonia.com/us/footprint.

it imperative to address these issues throughout the supply base to truly achieve ESR goals. It is also the supply base that poses the greatest threat to the brand reputation of many companies. Toyota, for example, has experienced several quality issues in recent years that led to product recalls and damaged the carmaker's reputation as a quality leader. But all of these events resulted from defective parts provided by suppliers.

To help their companies achieve their objectives, CPOs should step up to become the conscience keeper on ESR issues. This does not mean that CPOs should become "ESR directors," but rather that they can and should be the driving forces in cross-functional efforts to give their organizations a competitive edge through the response to ESR. CPOs should be accountable for these efforts because they are in a pivotal position to help the company achieve its ESR goals and use ESR partnerships to meet at least some procurement targets.

Success will require building new capabilities that enable procurement organizations to drive the ESR agenda internally and externally, make greater use of analytics, and strengthen their relationships with suppliers.

Enhance Capabilities to Drive the Company's ESR Agenda

To step up to their role in the ESR arena, CPOs need to develop a deep understanding of ESR issues and their internal and external impacts. For example, a global industrial conglomerate has launched initiatives to substantially reduce CO_2 emissions across its entire value chain, including its suppliers and customers, as well as its own emissions. As part of this initiative, it cut overall annual CO_2 emissions by roughly 320 million tons— an amount equal to the total annual CO_2 emissions of Berlin, Delhi, Hong Kong, Istanbul, London, New York, Singapore, and Tokyo combined. What are the capabilities required to fill this role? CPOs must be in a position to represent their companies in relevant external forums and industry bodies to shape the playing field and address ESR challenges. From there, they may connect further with key stakeholders of the regulatory environment and help drive their companies' ESR lobbying efforts. To be effective in these external interactions, CPOs must exhibit the internal credibility to drive ESR-influenced decision making—for example, with regard to the sourcing footprint, product design, or manufacturing.

Develop Analytical Approaches and Tools

To drive more informed business decisions, leading procurement organizations will need to embed a suite of approaches and tools to systematically analyze and assess ESR impacts.

To shift from decisions made on the basis of a gut feeling to quantitative decision making on ESR topics, CPOs will need to expand their existing suite of analytical tools. For example, the toolkit to assess the total cost of ownership needs to be enhanced to support decisions based on the total impact of ownership (TIO). The TIO toolkit should help quantify the additional costs, associated risks, and potential value opportunities for sourcing decisions.

To start developing the TIO mind-set and toolkit, companies need to make their supply chain fully transparent. This will be enabled by both technology and mandatory supplier disclosure requirements. The "farm to fork" traceability of products and services can be made possible by strong partnerships with suppliers beyond the tier 1 supply base and by making ESR elements a key criterion in supplier performance management. This transparency will help identify the direct costs, risks, and value opportunities created by the relevant ESR factors.

After they create transparency, companies will need to prioritize the most critical elements and assess the overall size of the risk or opportunity. They will need to develop advanced analytical models to measure the life-cycle impact of sourcing decisions. Procurement must collaborate closely with product development, marketing, and suppliers to understand potential changes to products and services and to ensure that these changes have the intended effect on the TIO. All these activities must be linked into the strategic sourcing process, where the costs, risks, and value at stake are being systematically assessed and balanced in the course of making sourcing decisions.

Forge Deeper Relationships across the Supply Chain

As companies focus on increased traceability for key commodities, procurement will need to go beyond tier 1 suppliers and develop relationships with tier 2 and tier 3 suppliers.

ESR aspects should be explicitly considered at each step in the supplier management life cycle, from vendor selection and development to ongoing management and review. Suppliers must be required to provide ESR and supply chain disclosures and participate in regular audits and reviews on ESR aspects. Greater transparency in the supply chain will allow procurement to identify risks and opportunities not only for tier 1 suppliers but also further upstream. Companies should increasingly and proactively use this transparency to offer support to the suppliers and the suppliers' suppliers. This can be done in a variety of ways, such as tier 2 or tier 3 sustainability audits, specific consultations and advice on ESR issues and value-generating opportunities, and assessments of ESR practices. The sustainability team should be responsible for these activities throughout the supply chain, and not limit the activities to tier 1 suppliers.

Develop Broader External Relationships

For procurement professionals, the world is evolving from a linear buyer-supplier relationship to a complex network of stakeholders. Unlocking full value from ESR-related initiatives requires procurement to develop relationships with multiple stakeholders—including suppliers, customers, industry bodies, governments, NGOs, and special-interest groups. For example, Kraft Foods has been working with the Rainforest Alliance to promote the sustainable sourcing of coffee beans. The Rainforest Alliance has helped to ensure a high-quality supply of coffee by teaching farmers the practices that comply with strict ESR standards.

Procurement must identify and participate in forums or collaborate with organizations relevant to the key products and services procured. These efforts should help shape future industry standards, provide support to groups lobbying for favorable regulatory changes, and influence groups to promote company strategies. This requires CPOs and their teams to develop deep content knowledge. They must also build new skills and capabilities to develop new, broader networks, communicate with the target audience, influence decision making, and manage a complex ecosystem of relationships.

■ ■ ■

Creating value from ESR requires systematic and comprehensive considerations of the issues and clear decision making with regard to trade-offs and strategic direction. A company's future success will depend on its ability to integrate ESR into its procurement and corporate strategies, build the right capabilities in its procurement function, and use the right set of tools to support decision making. Procurement must seek to become:

- The owner of the new, broader definition of total impact of ownership, encompassing nontraditional costs stemming from environmental (CO_2, water, waste); social (corporate social responsibility, local content, minority business); and regulatory (taxes, tariffs) issues.
- The expert on the business impact of ESR issues, possessing the ability to identify opportunities and threats for the company.
- An active contributor to the company's efforts to influence and shape government interventions.
- The shaper and priority setter for the sustainability agenda of the company and its suppliers: the corporate conscience keeper.

By now, CPOs should have given thought to which of the five topics we explored are the most relevant for their company—and which specific topics should be added to the CPO's 2020 agenda. Reflecting on this emerging aspiration, it becomes clear that getting there will require real change. In the next chapter, we explore how CPOs should think about their road map to Procurement 20/20, and how to initiate change.

PART 3

The Road Map to Procurement 20/20

CHAPTER 8

Getting Ready for Real Change: Steps for Starting the Journey toward Procurement 20/20

It's one thing to grasp the scope, immediacy, and impact of the five major trends. It's entirely another to respond in the right ways.

Granted, chief procurement officers (CPOs) are not strangers to change. Most have been through their share of cost-reduction campaigns; many have launched and run far-reaching supplier-consolidation programs. But though the traditional approach of category management discussed earlier remains relevant and valuable, the kind of transformation to supply entrepreneurship implicit in this book is much larger.

What's required is a holistic approach to change—a broad, sustained, and coordinated initiative that involves fundamental changes to the organization's strategy, structures, operating systems, capabilities, and culture. Such an initiative can take several years, regularly involves many business functions, and demands unwavering time and attention from senior executives. Put simply, CPOs must begin mapping out a detailed change-management program if they expect procurement to be one of the organization's strongest strategic contributors by the end of this decade.

Change management is, however, notoriously fragile. Many CPOs have no doubt seen—and perhaps experienced firsthand—representative examples of the 70 percent failure rate that McKinsey research has found to be typical of major transformations. Change fatigue can be especially damaging as employees ignore what they perceive to be the latest management notion, and their resistance can exacerbate workplace insecurity and encourage a return to business-as-usual behaviors. Thus, procurement leaders cannot treat change management as if it were another short-term project: It must be viewed as a stringent business discipline in its own right.

To help companies significantly improve the odds of achieving successful transformation, we have identified change guidelines and processes. These were gleaned from research performed over more than 10 years of helping companies implement major transformations and more than three years of working with organizational change experts, academics, and business leaders. Our findings are augmented by McKinsey's Organizational Health Index (OHI), a proprietary database containing organizational health data from 750,000 leaders across 650 organizations.

The findings demonstrate that the key to a successful change-management program lies in placing equal emphasis on two elements: a company's business performance and its organizational health. It's a tricky balance. Crafting initiatives that propel financial and operational results is something that business leaders understand. But it's not always obvious how crucial it is to cultivate organizational health as well. That point is easily overlooked because traditional metrics don't readily measure the development and evolution of the people-oriented aspects of change. The proof of why it's so important to get the balance right? A 2010 McKinsey survey of more than 2,500 senior executives whose organizations had undergone major transformations found that those initiatives that focused on both performance and organizational health were nearly three times as successful as those that focused on performance alone.

Our longtime studies of successful change management reveal five key steps that concurrently address business performance and organizational health: aspire to a clear vision, assess your current performance, architect the change program, act to deliver the program, and advance the changes so that they become embedded in the fabric of your organization. We explore these steps in this chapter.

It is not our intention to deliver a detailed treatise on change management, but we do intend to provide the tips necessary to enable CPOs and their management teams to take change management seriously. Here, then, is a prescriptive look at the foundational steps.

Aspire to a Clear Procurement Vision

The first step in any journey is deciding where to go. Your transformation program will be unique to your organization. It will potentially address the five megatrends we have outlined in previous chapters, but there are likely other themes that are relevant to your specific industry and company. Consequently, your journey will start from a very individual definition of your vision for procurement over the next three to five years.

Define the Opportunities Most Relevant to You

Your procurement organization cannot be all things to all people, so you must focus with laserlike precision on identifying the opportunities that are relevant to your industry, company, and organization and that will deliver the most to your bottom line.

That means that not all of the five megatrends outlined earlier in this book will apply in your case. Different issues affect different industries. Let's look at some examples.

The *consumer goods sector* has to continue managing the ever-increasing pressure on margins and continued high volatility in input prices. This will mean that cost reduction will continue to be important, but it will be far from sufficient. The procurement vision will need to include portfolio levers comprising (or combining) several of the key themes we have elaborated on in this book. Effective design to value will rapidly become a core part of the agenda; companies will far more frequently update product recipes and packaging, shifting swiftly to better take advantage of consumer preferences. Global sourcing strategies are driven even more by scarcity and volatility of key raw materials (this is the case, for example, for food and beverage manufacturers). End-to-end value chain optimization is key on the agenda for most of the global consumer companies—when managing product and brand complexity, for instance—using customer insights to develop internally or source innovation externally. We also see that many consumer players will establish even more control over raw-material costs through more upstream influence (for example, with farmer development programs). Leveraging big data will become even more important for consumer goods manufacturers, as they parse retail data in even more detail. Value creation through environment-friendly efforts and social responsibility measures is rising, with more public attention to upstream supply chain issues, including labor rates and treatment. Consumer procurement organizations and packaged-goods companies will have to play a more integrated role across the value change to enable and drive change more effectively and become a core value-creating function by the end of this decade.

The *retail sector* will have to find answers to the Great Global Rebalancing. In emerging markets, the retail sector is formalizing into national chains, while in the West footprints are shrinking and moving away from hypermarkets to smaller formats, driven by urbanization and online growth. Customers demand integrated multichannel shopping, which in turn, through big data and the global grid, creates massive opportunities for retailers to do a better job of predicting and fulfilling consumer demand. Consumers are being more demanding in terms of health, social responsibility, and environmental considerations that retailers need to address through sustainable sourcing models, supply chain transparency, and proper management of social media channels, as we explored in Chapter 7.

The *telecommunications sector* is figuring out how to establish 4G bandwidth effectively and to develop winning business models in the battle for cloud computing. More and more, telecommunications solutions involve making software-enabled versus hardware-enabled choices. So procurement teams must become increasingly adept at understanding the economics and costs associated with the hardware and software solutions they buy, leveraging advanced analytic tools, as discussed in Chapter 5. Moreover, the telecommunications value chain is disaggregating. Western carriers are moving away from buying hardware "boxes" from vendors, choosing instead to build their own networks and moving toward sourcing end-to-end turnkey solutions for new technology rollouts. This is a model that several emerging-market telecoms have already applied successfully. Procurement thus has a unique opportunity to help define what is still core to the company's operations (versus noncore) and to help establish and orchestrate the relevant external value chains and provider relationships. Last, considering that Chinese companies such as Huawei have by now assumed an innovation leadership role—measured in number of patents filed—telecoms need to consider how to partner and integrate with emerging-market players to tap future innovations and technologies.

The *pharmaceutical sector* is suffering from dwindling R&D effectiveness. Drugs worth 40 percent of global pharma revenues will lose patent protection by 2015 while health-care buyers are getting increasingly sophisticated in optimizing buying and reimbursements and emerging-market players are posing increasing competition. Overall demand for pharmaceutical companies' products is fundamentally shifting to emerging markets in line with the Great Global Rebalancing, and 70 percent of consumers in these markets belong to low-income segments, elevating the need for low-cost pharma business models. Pharmaceutical companies are already responding and shifting lower-value activities to lower-cost providers, especially in manufacturing. A procurement vision for pharma must at minimum address these changing business models, advocate better end-to-end provider management, and respond to the necessity to source more knowledge and intellectual property from external parties, all within the specific quality and regulatory boundaries of the industry.

The *oil and gas and energy sectors* are heavily impacted by the exploration of shale gas, major changes in the energy landscape from nuclear to renewable in line with the new economic drivers, increased local content requirements, and significant shifts in the power balance along the value chain. Procurement functions will need to deal with new suppliers, new technologies, and new legislative complexity. Government regulations also require procurement functions in the *financial institutions sector* to work closely with the risk management group to ensure compliance and to quickly identify and mitigate exposure to vendor risks, impacting total impact of ownership (explored in Chapter 7). The latter trend is also impacting the *aerospace sector*, which is leveraging tax breaks and subsidies in some countries as several nations encourage local aerospace development and manufacturing. Having an agile and dynamic supplier footprint, as described in Chapter 6, is key to supporting the rising opportunities, and procurement should also be the scout for these.

The procurement upshot: Each CPO must be able to marry the opportunities and issues pertaining to his or her company's industry with the company's individual needs and translate the resultant coupling into a clear procurement vision that propels the company forward. This vision-setting process can be driven only by the CPO. But what are the elements of that process? In addition to business foresight that incorporates the trends most affecting your industry, your vision should be based on the factual evidence that supports those trends, as well as on the strategy and needs expressed by your company at large.

Focus on the Medium Term

Initially, how high should you set your aspiration? Most successful change efforts define a medium-term future for each element of the transformation. Having a sense of where you want to be in three to five years gives you the immediacy, urgency, and tangibility you need to inspire stakeholders, set a rapid pace for change, break through resistance, and motivate the entire organization. We find that many leaders actually embark on their change journeys with a medium-term future in mind, and they fill in the details of their long-term vision along the way.

For instance, in 2009, the CPO of a major North American hospital system realized that even though the quality of medical supplies being produced in low-cost countries had risen significantly, those products still cost much less than the same products made in the United States. But, because that North America–based procurement organization lacked the skills to look outside the United States, the company hadn't taken advantage of the opportunity. To improve profitability radically, the procurement organization needed to take a global perspective.

To do so, the CPO developed a vision for establishing a global sourcing center in a low-cost region. The center was staffed with procurement leaders who had deep expertise in the local market as well as the know-how to move projects forward in a U.S. setting. The ultimate goals were first to cut costs by identifying products that could replace their U.S. counterparts on a one-for-one basis, and later to identify local products that could be used in the U.S. hospital. The CPO carefully designed a three-year program that would accommodate anticipated resistance from senior managers and clinicians. His goal at the end of the three-year period was simply to have the sourcing center fully staffed and its people trained in functional and leadership concepts, ready to generate sustainable results—an ambitious but achievable goal.

Now more than halfway through its change journey, the hospital system has accomplished more than expected. It has successfully established one global sourcing center and is expanding its reach into additional low-cost locations. Initial success in sourcing products that were low on physicians' preference lists has helped established a track record that now permits the organization to move into more highly engineered products for greater savings.

Set Stretch Performance and Organizational Health Goals

If your organization is to deliver lasting results, it must set stretch goals for both business performance (the financial and operational results the organization delivers for stakeholders) and organizational health (the ability to align, execute, and renew itself and sustain exceptional performance over time).

By definition, stretch goals are tough but achievable. They should inspire a new mind-set and create energy. Consider how President Kennedy's goal of putting a man on the moon inspired the aerospace industry in the 1960s and how the quest of automotive original equipment manufacturers (OEMs) to develop the "1-liter car" (100 kilometers per liter of fuel) inspires vehicle developers today. Most organizations, whether they are strugglers or top performers, have more headroom than they think before their goals become unattainable. Suppose you, the CPO of a North America–based organization, are kept busy with operational order fulfillment rather than strategic sourcing. If you were to tell your staff that you were planning to make the organization into an end-to-end value-chain orchestrator, that message would likely be met with skepticism, apathy, and perhaps even outright resistance. You don't get the change results you want simply by separating the strategic and tactical work for the buyers.

Suppose instead that you set a goal of becoming the leader in strategic category management in your industry, simultaneously teaming up with

the COO to support his or her quest to outsource more internal operations to external providers. You would build the required strategic sourcing
capabilities and would be deeply involved in some concrete make-or-buy
decisions and outsourcing projects. By establishing such a foundation first,
you would ensure that the stretch goal of becoming an end-to-end value-
chain orchestrator would present a more practical objective—something
that could be achieved over a reasonable time frame.

Performance goals are generally understood, but many organizations
struggle to understand organizational health goals. Consider a company
whose vision is to drastically reduce the time to market of new product
innovations by using IT-enabled collaboration with suppliers (a concept
referenced in Chapter 5). For these IT-enabled tools to have real impact,
the company needs procurement leaders whose position is well integrated
with the needs of both the technical and commercial organizations, as
well as the supply base. Those leaders have to understand the various parties' data, intellectual property, and confidentiality needs. Together with IT,
they must be able to translate those needs into software requirements for
external vendors. They also must be skilled at influencing senior executives, over whom they have no authority, urging them to act on the benefits that the tools deliver. This level of organizational health is what helps
an organization achieve its vision beyond the short term.

Generally speaking, for many procurement organizations, good health
means that their professionals are truly perceived as peers by the main
stakeholders, that they are fully embedded in the cross-functional teams,
and that they are involved early on in the product development process. A
position in a healthy procurement organization is not a dead end. Instead,
procurement professionals rotate regularly and move into other functions,
and the organization attracts internal talent.

How should your company gauge whether it is on track during this
phase of the transformation? The outcome of this step should be a company-
specific procurement vision that is bold, that takes into account the primary
themes your industry and company are facing, and that is aligned with
your company's business strategy. That vision should be clearly defined on
the basis of the three to five metrics most critical to your company's and
your procurement organization's situation. It must be supported by a broad
leadership coalition within procurement and also outside.

Assess Your Current Performance

After preparing a clear vision of what the procurement organization must
look like in the future, it's necessary to see where the organization stands

today. A candid assessment of the gap between present and future lays the groundwork for development of the skills, knowledge, and relationships that can propel the organization forward. There are two steps to this assessment: determining the performance and health capabilities that will help you achieve your vision and evaluating the status of those capabilities today.

Identify the Capabilities You Need to Succeed

The skills in which you need to invest will depend on your procurement vision. While elevating some skills up to industry parity will be adequate in many cases, some procurement organizations will need to make much bigger investments if they are to be able to field truly strategic skills.

For example, if your vision is to become an end-to-end orchestrator of the value chain, you will, at a minimum, need deep skills in supply market analysis, make-versus-buy determinants, benchmarking, and supplier performance management. If the need is to build an agile procurement organization that ensures continuous supply to your operations despite raw-material scarcity, you'll need capabilities in, for instance, advanced risk management, flexible supplier contracting, make-versus-buy decisions, hedging, and product design.

Of course, if your organization is to be able to enact change, it will need more than just performance capabilities. Its organizational health will depend on developing and promoting capabilities such as problem solving, the ability to influence senior management, and collaboration with the business units. Even more advanced skills will be needed depending on your specific vision; agile procurement, for example, calls for a highly refined ability to embrace and execute change rapidly.

Last but not least, it's a good idea to benchmark the capabilities needed against those found in industries that already excel at your vision. For instance, banks and insurance companies have employed sophisticated risk-management techniques for decades. The high-tech sector is the gold standard for outsourcing a significant part of the value chain. And consumer packaged-goods companies have marketed and sourced their products and innovations from low-cost countries for many years.

Determine the Strengths and Weaknesses of Your Employees

To architect a transformation appropriate for your organization, you'll need to conduct an inventory of your employees' capabilities against those that you've deemed critical for your procurement transformation. The key is to be rigorous, to base your assessment on facts, and to ensure you've included an analysis of the mind-set—that is, the organizational health—of your employees in addition to an understanding of their performance capabilities. Let's consider the aforementioned agile procurement example: If your employees are resistant to change, they will not act with the speed and preemptive agility required to avoid a factory shutdown that could follow a flood or a supplier's unexpectedly becoming insolvent, and things will inevitably go back to the way they had always been.

Determine the Strengths and Weaknesses of the Procurement Institution as a Whole

Strengths and weaknesses are institutional as well as personal. What good is it to develop flexible contracting skills if your leadership team cannot make decisions rapidly? What if the organization's perception of procurement is so poor that cross-functional leaders do not trust that its proposals are based on fact?

Our Global Purchasing Excellence (GPE) research has identified four key dimensions of procurement excellence, which were discussed in Chapter 1. With regard to your new vision, consider assessing two of these dimensions in greater detail: the integration and alignment with key stakeholders and the structures and systems of the organization.

Regarding the first dimension, ask yourself: Can I honestly say that key leaders across the company express faith that we can achieve our vision for procurement? The perspectives of the key leaders will, to a large extent, determine whether you are successful in transforming the organization. You won't get far without your stakeholders' active support. If you lack their support, you have to consider whether you're recruiting leaders with the right level of education and leadership skills, whether you're approaching the training of your organization appropriately, and whether you're successfully developing your leaders to take on roles of greater magnitude.

You must also address critical questions regarding structures and systems. Do you have the right cross-functional steering bodies in place to support making controversial decisions quickly and with the right expertise? Are the right metrics in place to support your vision? Will it be possible to measure the impact of this new vision and create positive momentum? Whereas the previous step looks at the competencies of any given buyer, this step looks at the competency and character of the collective organization to make forward progress.

Let's look at an example of the appropriate structures and systems. During the category transformation of a major German automotive OEM, the COO and the global head of R&D (both direct reports to the CEO) held biweekly progress reviews. Category teams presented their ideas, and the group made immediate decisions in somewhat heated—always fact-based—discussions. Both leaders showed visible signs of commitment: They were part of the kickoff for each new category wave, visited the teams in their optimization war rooms and showed real interest, and celebrated the successes with the teams. This tight steering enabled a 10 percent cost reduction across the entire external spend base during a period of rising commodity prices.

By the end of the assessment process, you should have a "people cube"—a compilation of the strengths and training needs for each of the employees whom you expect to involve in the transformation. You should know which of your existing capabilities will help you meet your goals and which need work. You should understand the mind-sets that will contribute to the program's success and the three to five specific aspects that you will need to fix (so that they won't undermine your initiatives). And you will certainly need to know what changes you need to make to your structures and systems to properly support change.

Architect the Change Program

Now that you know where you want to go and where you are today, you need to determine how to get there. Company leaders tell us this is the hardest part of transforming an organization. We have found that the following factors are common building blocks of almost every effective transformation architecture.

Executive Mandate

A mandate from the CEO is essential to the support of a bold vision, as we have already shown in our discussion of different trends in the previous chapters. You will need an initial mandate from the CEO so that you can assume the role of the convener of company-wide footprint considerations, as illustrated in Chapter 3, or as the orchestrator of the end-to-end value chain, as explained in Chapter 4. As a CPO, you have to involve the CEO not just in the development of and alignment with your vision but also in communicating your mandate for change.

This is critical for a few reasons. First, the engagement of the CEO will ensure that your vision is, from the very start, in sync with overall corporate strategy. It probably will not be effective if, for example, your vision calls for innovation sourcing in emerging economies when your CEO's focus is on improving local business spend as part of a social responsibility push. Second, an involved CEO has an ownership stake in the transformation and its success. Third, if you, the CPO, are championing this transformation as one of the company's top priorities, you must have the CEO's commitment. Lacking an equivalent level of commitment would send a mixed message that could easily derail the program. Last, the CEO is in a position to influence other senior leaders, encouraging them to support your change initiative even if it encroaches on what they consider to be their turf.

The more stakeholders involved, the more important the CEO's mandate will be. As initial successes start to roll in, you can expect a beneficial snowball effect. Your organization's credibility will grow, expanding your mandate to make even larger changes.

Initiative Portfolio Management

Let's say that you're the CPO of a high-tech company whose top management team wants to establish corporate social responsibility as a key priority, as discussed in Chapter 7. There are likely more initiatives to undertake than can be resourced. So in the short term, global supplier audits may need to be conducted to ensure that the laws and social norms of the home country or region are not violated. It may even be necessary to effect a wholesale change in strategy, turning to celebrity talent sourcing—that is, hiring big-name procurement specialists to foster the public perception the company wants to convey. At the same time, it can be helpful to launch a government-lobbying effort with the aim of imposing stricter environmental standards across the industry—standards that your company already upholds in its sourcing processes.

Overall, you will need to identify the many initiatives that can help you reach your vision, select and prioritize them according to your company's risk levels and resourcing, and then manage them together as a portfolio of initiatives.

To help devise a holistic set of initiatives, you can weigh each of these initiatives against time and familiarity. The grid that this exercise produces will reveal at a glance whether the initiatives are balanced. A balanced portfolio has initiatives that target short-, medium-, and long-term impact and includes both radical innovations and incremental improvements. The keys are to guard against fragmenting a change program across too many initiatives and to weigh the cost of money and resources against expected risks and rewards.

Stakeholder Alignment

The most successful procurement officers don't focus on creating value only for their internal customers—they do so for all of their stakeholders inside and outside the company.

For changes to take root, you'll need to make champions of the different groups you work with. That's no small task given that you may be asking functions to change the way they operate or to surrender some of their flexibility and autonomy. Imagine trying to assess the value of engineering outsourcing if the head of engineering is not convinced of the potential value associated with that move and doesn't see how it might help the engineering organization launch products faster.

You can align stakeholders in many ways. First, consider appointing business leaders from other functions as sponsors of your initiatives. How much more powerful would your outsourcing initiative be if the head of engineering were being held accountable for the same goals? You can establish transformation councils that include key stakeholders to make major decisions and resolve problems. You might also look at staffing your initiative team with cross-functional team members to get their input and engagement. Additionally, you might consider rotational programs that bring high-performing talent into procurement, even if only temporarily, to ensure the dissemination of procurement's goals and mind-set throughout the company, in addition to the fresh procurement thinking that rotational programs are intended to provide to various functions as talent rotates into their spheres.

Winning Over the Organization

A transformation program cannot succeed—no matter how carefully it has been crafted—if you cannot convince people that it has value and persuade them to help it take root. According to McKinsey's research, the two main reasons for the failure of most change-management programs are employee resistance and unproductive management behavior. Here are three building blocks to help you influence the rest of the organization.

A COMPELLING CHANGE STORY Once you've created and communicated your aspirations for procurement's performance and its organizational health, you should ask yourself, "Can my buyers, internal stakeholders, and suppliers truly say that they know what is expected of them and that they agree with it and want to support it?"

When you develop the change story for your organization, you should start with where your organization is now, including details about what is working, and then map out where it's going and how it will get there. Most important, you should talk about what the changes will mean for the people affected in your organization. Last, you should describe how the organization will know that it is succeeding.

The CPO of a large hospital system created a compelling vision and change story with the active support of his CEO, CFO, and COO. He rented a local sports stadium to kick off the program. Together with the top 50 people in the company, the CPO presented his appeal for change in a manner that was relevant to the organization, and key leaders across his company showed their solidarity. The program had the look and feel of a professional sports event, including a display of the goals for the organization on the scoreboard.

Externally, you'll want to engage the affected suppliers with a tailored version of your change story, outlining the goals of the transformation and its likely impact on them. Be sure that everyone inside your organization understands the change story before talking about it outside the company. You'll want others in your organization to be prepared to address questions from your suppliers—and to speak with one voice.

ROLE MODELING People change when they see their role models change. The top team must undergo a visible transformation and begin behaving in ways that demonstrate the type of mind-set and behaviors they expect.

The CPO might consider having the CEO and the head of R&D convey the change story to the procurement organization, explaining what it will mean for them. The CPO can also have high-ranking R&D and business unit leaders write their own versions of the change story for deployment to their line organizations. Another tactic is to ask marketing or business unit leaders, who may be on the hook for delivering new products faster, to attend key business reviews at which they can promote your vision in addition to their own.

On an initiative level, select and nurture influential leaders—professionals with wide circles of personal contacts who respect and emulate them—regardless of their functions or positions.

REINFORCEMENT MECHANISMS Next, consider whether the organization's formal mechanisms reinforce the shifts in mind-set that are expected. To make sure the organization's mechanisms are reinforcing the shifts, procurement organizations need to tie their performance and organizational health to rewards and consequences, adjusting their management processes, structures, and systems accordingly.

The rewards don't have to be financial. Public and private recognition, such as a write-up in a transformation newsletter, can go a long way toward building organizational morale. And small but unexpected rewards, including employee dinners and gift vouchers, can pack a disproportionate punch, because they are seen as tokens of respect or appreciation.

A large food company applied these principles as it went through a merger with another company that had markedly different cultural norms. The food company faced significant increases in raw-material costs along with economic pressure to make significant efficiency gains as a benefit of the merger.

To kick-start change, the leaders of the company's procurement organization completely overhauled its remuneration package. One company had not established a variable compensation plan, while the other had a payment system under which a buyer could earn the equivalent of up to two months' salary on the basis of criteria that were not linked to procurement performance. The food company's top team revised this package so that all managers involved in the transformational change program could earn up to nine months of additional salary on the basis of project performance and individual participation. This approach forced instinctive cooperation and stiffened managers' resolve to pursue opportunities that were right for the company. As a result, the food company completed 50 mini-initiatives aimed at reducing costs in one year, instead of the 38 originally slated.

Capability Building

We have shown that all five megatrends offer the procurement organization significant opportunities to step up its game; however, the opportunities all require specialized skills that many procurement organizations will have to build first. Developing the necessary skills—both technical and leadership—is crucial to the success of a transformation and must be carefully architected to bridge the gap between the current assessment and the vision.

A few practical tips capture what is meant by "carefully architected." You cannot rely on a classroom environment alone. Adults learn best through a combination of hearing, seeing, and doing. So you'll need to combine brief classroom sessions with many interactive learning opportunities, along with on-the-ground applications of the lessons.

Moreover, employees need the opportunity—and the time—to practice in the real world after their training is over, both before and during your transformation. So in a situation like the flexible supply chain example described previously, the CPO should consider creating interactive simulations that let buyers see the impact of their sourcing decisions during a natural disaster. He or she could have the trainees solve problems related to a real and significant decision the initiative team might have to make, followed by a recommendation to the leadership team for moving forward. Then the CPO might require the team leader to report the results of the recommendation, making it easier to come up with a concrete measurement of the team's progress and to pinpoint what it has learned.

To architect the program, you will need a small group of people with expertise in communication, organizational health, capability building, and impact tracking. During this phase, you will know you're on the right path when you have created a balanced portfolio that includes quick wins that build momentum, medium-term initiatives that push the envelope, and long-term initiatives that foster more radical change. You will have teams comprising highly skilled and influential leaders, programs designed to develop the capabilities you need, and senior executives who are starting to perform their roles in concert with the change you're seeking.

Act to Deliver the Program

Now that you have designed the program, it is time to act. This phase is all about action and making certain that the program is rolled out with significant oversight during the first 100 days and that the hearts and minds of your employees are captured in ways beyond formal mechanisms.

It is critically important that you start with some successful lighthouse cases. Procurement leaders have to pilot the program cautiously before a full-scale rollout is attempted, ensuring that feedback is actively incorporated into the program design. You will need to identify the first subset of areas in which you will pilot the improvements. These areas can be selected on the basis of the greatest opportunity for impact, success, or stakeholder alignment to the transformation. If you were directing the corporate social-responsibility example, perhaps you would pilot your supplier audit program across companies in high-risk regions where you are certain to make impact, generating enthusiasm and support for the program. For global dynamic sourcing, you might seek out arbitrage opportunities and promote them.

The rollout can be designed to be linear or exponential or to have big-bang impact, depending on level of urgency, similarity across deployment areas, and available resources. To build accountability beyond formal mechanisms, you might consider a viral marketing program that will energize and excite your organization and will build the engagement of your cross-functional stakeholders.

Programs that motivate employees through communications and personal involvement are twice as likely to be considered extremely successful. This sense of ownership can be developed in two ways: through formal accountabilities given to leaders and with viral tactics that energize people within the company.

To develop formal accountabilities, begin at the top with an executive steering committee that includes yourself as the CPO and members of the senior executive team who can break through bottlenecks and keep the program on track. You will also need a small team of people charged with coordinating the program and tracking its progress.

Viral tactics can mobilize people to embrace the transformation. Consider creating videos you can show internally online or in the break room. These videos might showcase how, for instance, new risk-management practices prevent supply disruptions or how specific individuals identified innovation opportunities in emerging countries. Circulate a newsletter across the organization highlighting the progress toward the transformation goals.

Measurement is a constant in every area of business, but a transformation needs highly granular current data, because it must adapt to new challenges and opportunities as they emerge. It's the program management team's task to develop the right metrics. For example, if you are trying to mitigate your organization's exposure to volatility in raw-material availability and energy prices, you might consider the following metrics: overall exposure in a worst-case scenario, costs and volatility reduction per measure taken, and assessment of performance relative to a do-nothing scenario.

Advance the Changes

Even when CPOs have mastered the first four change steps, the journey will be far from over. In fact, it will have barely begun. The phase to advance the changes will focus on building the capacity for continuous improvement into the organization's DNA.

Building this capacity is a task that requires as much energy and focus as any other stage in a transformation. Continuous improvement is everyone's job, and companies that excel at it generally put certain people and groups—often former members of the program management—in charge of making it happen.

Several measures can help to get your organization into a continuous improvement mode, including establishing systems for sharing knowledge and best practices, systematically identifying and capturing opportunities for improvement, adopting methods of continuous learning, and cultivating dedicated expertise that can question the status quo.

Ultimately, the most important message for advancing change in your transformation to 2020 is to never stop adapting: The vision that you set for your organization today may require many course corrections if it is to be successful several years down the road.

■　■　■

In writing this chapter, it has not been our goal to lay out a detailed blue-print for successful change management. Our intent has been to define and describe some of the basic disciplines that we have seen foster success. Success is certainly within reach. But the urgency to act must come from you.

CHAPTER 9

Your Agenda Now

In many organizations across many industries, procurement has an opportunity to perform on a far higher plane. In fact, it has an *obligation* to do so.

Seizing that opportunity—meeting that obligation—is not just a question of stepping up to current best practice, laudable though that is. It's a question of fully understanding and proactively preparing adequate responses to the tectonic shifts facing business today—shifts that range from the explosion of useful data to the emerging economies' ascent up the value chain. In short, it is about moving from supply management to supply entrepreneurship.

The fundamental drivers of change are no longer in dispute. As noted early in this book, the decade ahead—actually, as far ahead as we can see—will be no less tumultuous. By 2020, procurement's role will have become even more important for sustaining constant supply, best cost, reduced volatility, faster and improved innovation, and clean corporate-brand image.

The time for casual discussion is over. Procurement's strategic role is no longer a topic reserved chiefly for conference panels and academic arguments. This is, without doubt, a time for action. Shareholders have a right to expect determined, directed, discrete action. CEOs and boards of directors who are not yet requiring that of their procurement leaders are themselves falling short.

So these are the big questions: What kinds of action? On what timetable? With what resources? According to what metrics? The specific answers to those questions are for you, as chief procurement officer, to determine with your leadership team. Our objective in writing this book has been to lay the groundwork for those decisions.

In the preceding pages, we have presented the key dimensions of procurement excellence in all sectors and shared practical advice for improving these foundational elements. We have provided clear perspectives on the five megatrends that will change the way we all do business in the decade ahead. We have detailed the impact these trends will have on your procurement function. And we have presented a framework for how you can redefine your own vision of procurement and how you can implement the required changes.

The timetable for many of those changes may be years long. Many of the necessary transformations of processes—and most of the cultural and behavioral shifts—will not happen overnight. But that does not excuse a languid approach to change. There has to be visible, tangible activity in the next quarter. Within the next 100 days, you should be able to give directional answers to the chief executive about all the major issues addressed in this book. A year from now, the CEO should be able to see many of the outcomes of your answers.

How soon can you promise those outcomes? Tomorrow is knocking on your door.

About the Authors

PETER SPILLER is a Principal in McKinsey's Frankfurt office and leader of the firm's Europe, Middle East, and Africa (EMEA) purchasing and supply management practice, serving clients in the automotive, telecommunications, and high-tech sectors on operations transformations and strategy.

NICOLAS REINECKE is a Tenured Expert Principal in McKinsey's Hamburg office. He is part of the EMEA operations leadership team, focusing on supply management and operations topics across industries and geographies.

DREW UNGERMAN is a Director in McKinsey's Dallas office and leads the firm's Americas purchasing and supply management practice. He advises clients across the health care value chain on strategy and operations.

HENRIQUE TEIXEIRA is a Principal in McKinsey's São Paulo office. He is the leader of the firm's Latin America purchasing and supply management practice and sourcing center.

Acknowledgments

This book would not have been possible without the generous support we received from colleagues who inspired and challenged us and provided examples of procurement's rapid evolution.

First and foremost, we would like to thank our clients and our colleagues in several of McKinsey's practices—in particular in Purchasing & Supply Management, Strategy, and Organization—as well as the McKinsey Global Institute.

Several colleagues deserve our special thanks: the global operations leaders, Bruce Simpson, Cornelius Baur, and Gernot Strube, and the global Purchasing and Supply Management conveners, Aurobind Satpathy and Jan Wüllenweber, for their overall guidance and support in making the book a reality; Michael Sohn, for his relentless efforts to ensure that all contributors were aligned on the project's goals; and Elizabeth John as well as Milan Prilepok for providing content, editing, and project management whenever and wherever needed.

We also thank our senior colleagues who led the development of content for the five megatrends: Oliver Schubert for the Great Global Rebalancing, Diego Barilla for the productivity imperative, Milan Prilepok for big data and the global grid, Michael Sohn for volatility as the new normal, and Tarandeep Ahuja and Kalit Jain for the new economic drivers.

Last, we want to thank John Kerr and his editorial colleagues for their assistance in editing the book and constructively challenging our insights.

Index

Acer, 57
Act to deliver the program, 153–154
Advance the changes, 154–155
Aerospace sector, 143
Africa, 23, 32, 35–37, 39
Agenda now, 157–158
Agile procurement, 91, 95, 97
  agile infrastructure, 114
  building steps, 105–106
  decision making speed and
    processes, 114
  development and implementation of
    cross-functional teams, 110–112
  key enablers, 113–115
  personnel dedication and skill
    sets, 113
  tools, 113
  uncertainty definition, 106–107
Airbus, 83
Airtel, 70
Alcatel-Lucent, 70
Amazon, 73
Anticipation, 95–96
Apple, 52, 60, 62–63, 65
Ariba, 78
Asia, 32, 36, 46, 121
Australia, 23, 123, 125

Bangladesh, 26, 36
Benchmarking, internal and external
  functions, 67
Big data, 73, 75, 82, 88
  global connectivity and possibilities
    and risk, 21
  procurement readiness, 21–22
  technical solutions to analyze, 86–87
Bloomberg, 77

BMW, 24, 55
Boeing, 38, 83
Brands, 55
Business acceleration, 55
Business model resilience, 108

Cameroon, 101
Canada, 42
Capabilities, 66–67, 84–85
  benchmark, 146
  and culture, 4, 6
  foundation building, 85–87
  target expansion and pilots, 87–89
Capability building, 152–153
Carbon dioxide (CO2) emissions, 132
Carbon emissions, 121
Carrefour, 38
Cash flow at risk (CFaR) analysis, 113
Category management and execution,
  4, 6–9
Category management performance
  cross-functional category team and
    steering governance, 11–12
  management approach, 12
  performance management, 12–13
Central Europe, 39
Centrally coordinated procurement
  function, 9
CEO mandate, 64–65
Change fatigue, 139
Change program, architect, 148–153
  executive mandate, 148–149
  initiative portfolio management, 149
  stakeholder alignment, 149–150
  winning over the organization,
    150–152
Change story, 150–151

Chief Procurement Officers (CPOs). *See* CPOs (Chief Procurement Officers)
Chile, 25
China, 15–17, 20, 23, 25, 31–32, 34, 36–40, 100, 121
Cisco Systems, 21
"Clean sheet" cost calculations, 79
Climate change, 25
Coca-Cola, 52, 129
Cocoa Plan, 129
Collaboration
  closeness and outcomes, 130–131
  internal, 9
  at scale, 76
Commoditization of functional excellence, 56–57
Commodity exchanges, 102
Commodity prices, 23–24
Company agenda capabilities, 132
Compliance, 82
Computing, 19
Confidentiality requirements, 83
Consumer goods sector, 141
Contract research organizations (CROs), 54
Cook, Tim, 62–63, 65
Cost of goods sold (COGS), 101, 105, 107
Cotê d'Ivore, 129
CPOs (Chief Procurement Officers)
  aspirations, 114–115
  capabilities, new, 66–69
  CEO mandate, 64–65, 148
  change management, 139–140
  vs. COO, 65
  coordination with others, 154
  definition, 68–69
  orchestral role, 64, 66
  relationships, 134
  reporting to CEO, 10
  stepping up, 63–71
  value added to key stakeholders, 66
Craigslist, 52
Credibility, 87
Cross-border capital flows, 20, 74
Cross-function integration
  enterprise, 113

Cross-functional category team and steering governance, 11–12
Cross-functional support for footprint decision making, 44–45
Cross-functionality, 96–97
Cross-sector consortium buying, 82–83
Currency options, 102

Data-driven decision making, 73–75
  capabilities to capture opportunities, 84–89
  enhanced data-driven decisions, 75–78
  procurement, opportunities in core activities and beyond, 78–84
Decision making speed and processes, 114
Deese, Willie, 64–65
Demand and downstream uncertainties, 107
Demand and specification management, 8
Democratic Republic of the Congo, 130
Design to cost, 103
Design to switchability, 103
Development of suppliers and ecosystems, 100–101
DHI, 98
Diageo, 101
Disaster risk management, 98
Disaster-response strategy, 105
Drivers of outsourcing
  greater availability of offerings, 56–57
  market pressures, 55–56
Drivers of procurement performance, 55–58
Dun & Bradstreet, 75
Dynamic footprint decisions, 42–43
  cross-functional support for footprint decision making, 44–45
  flexible supply chains to operationalize, 45–47
Dynamic sourcing, 33–36, 40–41, 99

Eastern Europe, 32, 36, 39, 46, 126
Economic factors. *See* Sourcing risk into competitive advantage
Economies of skill, 9–10

The Economist (magazine), 95
Electronic manufacturing service (EMS), 56
Emerging markets, 17–18, 23, 33–37, 39, 50
Employee motivation, 124
Employees' strength and weakness, 146–147
End-to-end value chain, 18, 46
Energy, 23
Energy requirements, volatility, 94
Enterprise resource planning (ERP), 21, 76
Environmental, social, and regulatory (ESR)
  company agenda capabilities, 132
  considerations, 118
  impacts measurement, 128
  issues, 24, 115, 120, 121, 126–128
E-procurement tools, 8
Ericsson, 69
European Brand Association (AIM PROGRESS), 130–131
European Union, 23, 39, 122
Executive mandate, 148–149
Export tariffs, 41
Exposure measurement, 107–108
External development relationships, 134–135
External event-driven uncertainties, 106
External provider
  integration, 67
  relationships, 67–68
External relationships, 128–129
  full supply chain focus, 129
  stakeholders and industry standards, 128–129

Facebook, 20
Fact base on ESR issues, 126–127
Factor cost, 54
Factor cost increases, 121
Failure modes and effects analysis (FMEA), 108
Financial hedging instruments, 102
Financial institutions sector, 143
Financial strength and shareholder agreement, 108–109

Finite element method (FEM), 108
Firstsource, 70
Flexibility into supplier and customer contracting, 101–103
Flexible supply chains to operationalize, 45–47
Flextronics, 46
Footprint opportunities, 44
Ford, 37
Forecasting and shaping of customer demand, 104
The Forest Trust (TFT), 118
Foundation building
  big data, technical solutions to analyze, 86–87
  talent, analytical, 85–86
Foxconn, 56–57, 63
France, 42
Frito-Lay, 37
Fujitsu, 105
Fukushima disaster, 96
Full supply chain focus, 129
Functional specialists, 51–54
  factor cost, 54
  operational scale, 54
  specialized skill, 54
Functional specifications, 103
Future market prices, 87
Futures and derivatives, 102

General Electric (GE), 16–17, 37
Germany, 37, 61, 147
Ghana, 39, 101
Global commodities, 24
Global connectivity and possibilities and risk, 21
Global eProcedure, 78
Global information, 74
Global Purchasing Excellence (GPE) research, 3–4, 8, 11, 50, 85, 92, 147
Global rebalancing
  emerging markets as innovation and talent, 17
  private consumption and cost innovation, 16–17
  procurement readiness, 17–18

Global rebalancing, sourcing footprint,
    31–33
  dynamic footprint decisions, 42–47
  dynamic sourcing, 33–36
  factors shaping, 36–37
Globalization, 56
Goals stretched, procurement and
    organizational, 144–145
Google Earth, 75
Google Maps, 75
Government activism, 121
Government regulations, 40–42
GPE research. *See* Global Purchasing
    Excellence (GPE) research
Great Global Rebalancing, 16–17,
    31–34, 41, 46, 121, 141–142
Greenpeace, 118, 120
Gross domestic product (GDP)
    growth, 74

Health care, 19
Hedges and hedging, 102
Heightened negotiation intelligence,
    79–80
Helix, 100
Henkel, 94
Hewlett Packard (HP), 112
Honda, 91–92
Honduras, 36, 96
Huawei, 17, 39, 70

IBM, 21, 70
Ikea, 32, 101
Impacts measurement, 128
Import tariffs, 40, 42
India, 16–17, 20, 23, 32, 38–40, 42,
    70–71, 101
Indonesia, 32, 36, 38, 41–42, 118
Industry norm elevation, 126
Industry structure improvement, 124
Information and global connectivity, 20–21
Information flows, 20
Information technology (IT), 8
  development, 39
  infrastructure and analytic
    capability, 111
  IT-enabled networking, 76

Initiative portfolio management, 149
InnoCentive, 57–58
Innovation, 84
  and advantages, 39
Integration and alignment, 6
Intel, 22
Internal collaboration, 9
International Union for
    Conservation of Nature
    (IUCN), 120
Internet Protocol (IP) phone
    subscribers, 69
Iran, 23
Iraq, 23
ISO 31000, 92
Issues, 24
Issues in procurement,
    119–120

Japan, 18, 34, 37–38, 91,
    94–95, 105
John Deere, 21
Just-in-time (JIT) supply, 46

Kennedy, John F., 144
Kenya, 39, 101
Key performance indicators (KPIs), 60,
    66–67, 70, 81, 85, 87
Key risks, 96
Knowledge-management
    processes, 10
Kraft Foods, 134

Labor rates, 107
Lafer, A. G., 52
Lanthanum, 100
Latin America, 36, 39
Lenovo, 37
Li & Fung, 99
London Metal Exchange, 102
Low-cost countries (LCCs), 79
Lufthansa, 94, 102

Magna Steyr, 55, 60
Maintenance, repair, and operations
    (MROs), 80
Malaysia, 42

Management
  approach, 12
  principles for productivity, 19
  quality of, 19
  skills, 68
Mandatory ESR consideration
  industry norm elevation, 126
  license for operation, 125
  new market access, 125
  tight market supply,
    125–126
Market fluctuations, 105
Market pressures
  business acceleration, 55
  globalization, 56
Market price volatility, 106
Market risk, 108
Markets, amplified volatility
  of, 23
Markets and products, new, 123
McKinsey, 3, 16
McKinsey Global Institute (MGI),
  16, 93
McKinsey global survey (2012),
  126, 128
McKinsey research, 19, 139
McKinsey's Organizational Health Index
  (OHI), 140
Megatrends, 25–27
  big data and the global grid,
    20–22
  great global rebalancing,
    16–18
  new economic drivers,
    25–26
  productivity imperative,
    18–20
  volatile new normal, 22–25
Mexico, 36–37, 39, 46
Middle East, 23
Modularity, 103
Monetization of propriety
  information, 84
Monte Carlo simulation, 108
Mphasis, 70
Multinational companies, 34
Munich Re, 94

Nature (magazine), 118
Negotiation capabilities
  enhanced negotiation scenario
    analyses, 80
  heightened negotiation intelligence,
    79–80
Nespresso, 120
Nestlé, 101, 118–119,
  125, 129
Nestlé Supplier Code, 119
New costs from ESR, 122
New market access, 125
New opportunities from ESR
  employee motivation, 124
  industry structure improvement, 124
  markets and products,
    new, 123
  quality and consistency
    improvement, 123
  total costs reductions, 123
Nicaragua, 36
Nielsen, 75
Nigeria, 39, 101
Nokia Siemens, 39
Nortel, 70
North America, 32, 143–144
Nortura, 21
NSN, 70

Oil and gas
  energy sector, 142–143
  reserves, 23
Open-source innovation
  continues, 84
Operational scale, 54
Opportunities relevant to
  industry/company/organization,
    141–143
Oracle, 78
Orchestration need for end to end
  value chain, 58–59
Organization
  assessment, 146
  capabilities benchmark, 146
Organizational health
  goals, 145

Original design manufacturers (ODMs),
    52, 56
Original equipment manufacturers
    (OEMs), 37, 56
Outsourcing offerings
    commoditization of functional
        excellence, 56–57
    greater availability of, 56–57
    standardization of IT and business
        processes, 57–58
Outsourcing risk mitigation, 58

Pakistan, 26, 101
Palm oil, 42
Panasonic, 22
Patagonia, 131
Performance, assessment of current, 146
    capabilities needed for success, 146
    employees' strength and weakness,
        146–147
    procurement institution weakness
        and strengths, 147–148
Performance management, 12–13
Personnel dedication and skill sets, 113
Perspective broadening, 106
Peru, 24
Pharmaceutical sector, 142
Philippines, 12, 25, 39
Physical hedging, 102
Porter's five forces, 43
Portugal, 46
Power for decisions across functions,
    43–44
Preemptive agility creation, 99–104
    design to switchability, 103
    development of suppliers and
        ecosystems, 100–101
    flexibility into supplier and customer
        contracting, 101–103
    forecasting and shaping of customer
        demand, 104
    uncertainties in future supply base,
        99–100
Presumptive procurement levers, 111
Private consumption and cost
    innovation, 16–17

Proctor & Gamble (P&G), 17, 52
Procurement, new model of agile
    anticipation, 95–96
    application software, 78
    benefits, 4–6
    comprehensive view, 97–99
    coping with ESR, 124–126
    cross functionality, 96–97
    functions, 86
    institution weakness and strengths,
        147–148
    natural role, 77–78
    new model of agile, 95–99
    opportunities in core activities and
        beyond, 78–84
    performance drivers, 3–13
    readiness, 17–22, 24–27
    road map to 20/20, 139–145, 148–155
    role, 59–60
    vision, 140–148
Productivity imperative, 51
    companies riding the waves, 69–71
    drivers, 55–58
    functional specialists, 51–54
    orchestration need, 58–59
    possibilities, 60–63
    procurement role, 59–60
    stepping up to the CPO role, 63–71
Public awareness, 120
Publishers' Database for Responsible
    Environmental Paper Sourcing
    (PREPS database), 129
Purchasing and alignment, 99

Qoros, 60–62
Quality and consistency improvement,
    123
Quanta, 56

Rainforest Alliance, 134
Rare earth elements, 100
Raw materials
    hedges, 102
    scarcity, 91
    volatility, 107
Recyclability, 103

Regulatory and social issues, 25–26
Regulatory factors. *See* ESR
Reinforcement mechanisms, 151–152
Relevant uncertainty definition
  exposure measurement, 107–108
  perspective broadening, 106
  range of risk, 109–110
  risk owner, 108–109
  risk quantification and response
    options, 107–110
  risk type definition, 106–107
  uncertainty analysis, 106
Reshoring, 37
Resource demand vs. supply, 23
Responsive agile procurement
    levers, 111
Retail sector, 141–142
Revenues per employee (RPE), 51
Reverse innovations, 39
Risk appetite, 109–110
Risk owner, 108–109
Risk-management services, 88
Risk(s)
  and compliance management, 83
  currency options, 102
  disaster risk management, 98
  global connectivity and possibilities, 21
  heightened, 122
  management and mitigation
    skills, 108
  management of, 114
  market risk, 108
  outsourcing risk mitigation, 58
  of overdependency, 62
  physical hedges, 102
  quantification and response options,
    107–110
  range of, 109–110
  raw-material hedges, 102
  risk type definition, 106–107
  set of, 107
  of supplier quality issues, 107
  supply chain risk, 40
  supply chain risk mitigation, 39–40
Role modeling, 151
Russia, 41–42

Saudi Arabia, 23
Scarcity of raw materials, 91
Seagate, 22
Sectors
  aerospace, 143
  consumer goods, 141
  financial institutions, 143
  oil and gas energy, 142–143
  pharmaceutical, 142
  retail, 141–142
  telecommunications, 142
Semcon, 60
Senior alignment sessions, 43
Sentiment analysis, 73
Serving local customers, 37–38
SGL Group, 24
Sharp, 22
Shell, 118
"Should cost" models, 79
Siemens, 125
Sierra Leone, 101
Singapore, 121, 127, 132
Single-source provider, 96
Skype, 52, 69–70
Smarteq, 46
Smith, Adam, 18
Social factors. *See* Economic drivers'
    impacts
Sony, 22, 94
Sourcing, 45
Sourcing at best cost, 36–37
Sourcing footprint, factors shaping,
    36–42. *In order as presented*
  sourcing at best cost, 36–37
  serving local customers, 37–38
  anchor points for company, 38–39
  innovation and advantages, 39
  supply chain risk mitigation, 39–40
  sustainability issues, 40
  dynamic sourcing, 40–41
  government regulations, 40–42
Sourcing footprints, 41–42, 45
South Africa, 35
South America, 32
South Asia, 23
South Korea, 39

Spain, 45–46
Specialized skill, 54
Specifications and demand, better
    management of
  benchmarking demand and
    specification, 81–82
  compliance ensured, 82
  true demand, 81
Stakeholder alignment, 68, 149–150
Stakeholders and industry standards,
    128–129
Standardization of IT and business
    processes, 57–58
Stora Enso, 102
Structures and systems, 4, 6
Supplier ecosystem, 101
Supplier portfolio, 99
Supply and upstream uncertainties, 106
Supply chain relationship development,
    133–134
Supply chain risk, 40
Supply chain risk mitigation, 39–40
Supply volatility, 104
The Sustainability Consortium
    (TSC), 126
Sustainability issues, 40
Sustainable Apparel Coalition, 129
Sustainable Sourcing Advisory Board
    (SSAB), 126
Sweden, 61
Switzerland, 121, 127
Synnex, 56
Synthetic hedging, 102
Systematic assessment of ESR
    issues, 128

Talent, analytical, 85–86
Talent as key asset, 6–7
Tamkivi, Sten, 69–70
Targeted expansion and pilots
  credibility gains, 87
  lessons from pilots, 87–88
  value by pilot expansion, 88
Tariffs
  export, 41
  import, 42–43

Technology leveraging, 131
Telecommunications sector, 142
Teleperformance, 70
Tesco, 21
Thailand
Thomson Reuters, 77
Tight market supply, 125–126
Time, 96–97
Time-to-market initiatives, 83
TomTom, 21
Total cost of goods sold
    (COGS), 107
Total cost of ownership (TCO), 126
  elements, 80
  model development, 113
  models, 45, 81
Total costs reductions, 123
Total impact of ownership (TIO), 126,
    133
Total-cost approach, 11
Total-cost-of-ownership
    methodology, 8
Toyota Prius, 100
Training program, 7
True demand, 81
TSMC, 51

Uncertainties in future supply base,
    99–100
Uncertainty analysis, 106
Unilever, 38, 125–126, 130
United States, 18, 23–24, 37, 39, 80, 83,
    95, 143

Value added to key stakeholders, 66
Value by pilot expansion, 88
Value chain, 59, 113
Venezuela, 23
Vietnam, 32, 36
Vodafone, 21
Volatility, 91
  changes, 98
  of demand vs. supply, 98
  energy requirements, 94
  era of greater, 93–95
Volkswagen, 24, 46

Wal-Mart, 95–96, 120, 126
Water scarcity, 23
Weather hedging, 102
Western Digital, 22
Winning over the organization
  capability building, 152–153
  change story, 150–151
  reinforcement mechanisms, 151–152
  role modeling, 151

Wistron, 57
World Trade Organization
  (WTO), 41
World Wildlife Fund (WWF),
  101, 129

Zara, 45–46
Zhou, Mark, 61–62
ZTE, 39